TABLE OF CONTENTS

An Ode to my Dad	4
Christianne Blenkin	9
Recovery to Discovery	13
The Art of Being a Role Model	19
The Interview	25
My Martial Art Influencers	29
Australia's Hidden Wing Chun Legacy	31
Introduction to Capoeira	36
West Coast Aikido Inspiration	50
Advancement in Japanese Martial Arts	51
How I Came to Learn Krav Maga	55
Kaiya Regan	59
Tiana	62
Martial Arts V's Self-defence	64
Matayoshi Kobudo	69
The Wisdom of Mr Keisuke Miyagi	75
Miyamoto Musashi	81
24 - The Martial Artist	86
Empowered by Ronda Rousey	87

Dear reader,

Welcome to our latest issue of Martial Arts Magazine Australia. As I reflect on the diverse and inspiring collection of articles in this edition, I'm struck by the profound impact of role models in martial arts.

From the wisdom of Mr. Miyagi to the real-life inspirations like Ronda Rousey, this issue highlights how influential figures shape not just our techniques, but our character and approach to life. The article on "The Art of Being a Role Model" beautifully encapsulates this, reminding us that true martial arts mastery extends far beyond physical prowess to encompass qualities like humility, integrity, and compassion. We see this exemplified in stories like that of Grandmaster Gregory Choi, whose dedication to preserving and passing on the legacy of Wing Chun demonstrates the importance of honoring tradition while adapting to the present. Similarly, the profile of young Kaiya showcases how early exposure to positive role models in martial arts can nurture exceptional talent and character.

The pieces on historical figures like Miyamoto Musashi offer timeless insights, showing how the principles of martial arts philosophy continue to resonate centuries later. Meanwhile, articles on modern practices like Brazilian Jiu-Jitsu and Capoeira illustrate the evolving nature of martial arts and their ability to empower practitioners across cultures.

I'm particularly impressed by the range of voices and experiences represented in this issue. From instructors sharing their teaching philosophies to practitioners reflecting on their personal journeys, each story offers a unique perspective on the transformative power of martial arts.

As editor, I'm proud to present such a rich tapestry of content that not only informs but inspires. These articles remind us that in martial arts, we are all constantly learning and growing, and that the best practitioners are those who not only excel in their discipline but also strive to be positive influences in their communities.

Thank you to all our contributors for sharing their knowledge and experiences. And to our readers, I hope this issue motivates you to reflect on the role models in your own martial arts journey and perhaps inspires you to become one for others.

Train hard, stay humble, and enjoy the read.

Vanessa McKay

COPYRIGHT

All content published in MAMA (Marital Arts Magazine Australia), including articles, images, and other media, is the property of the magazine and is protected by copyright law. The author retains the copyright to their individual work, but by submitting their work to MAMA, they grant the magazine an exclusive, perpetual, and irrevocable license to publish and distribute their work in all formats, including print, digital, and online media. No part of MAMA may be reproduced, distributed, or transmitted in any form or by any means, including photocopying, recording, or other electronic or mechanical methods, without the prior written permission of the magazine.

MAMA respects the intellectual property rights of others and expects its contributors and readers to do the same. If you believe that your copyrighted work has been used in a way that constitutes copyright infringement, please contact MAMA immediately. Additionally, any use of MAMA trademarks, including the magazine's name and logo, without prior written authorization from the magazine, is prohibited.

MAMA strives to showcase original and unique content, and as such, does not accept any submissions that have been previously published or that are under consideration by other publications. By submitting their work to MAWA Magazine, the author confirms that their work is original and has not been published or submitted elsewhere.

In addition, MAMA reserves the right to edit all submissions for grammar, style, and clarity, and to reject any submission that does not adhere to the magazine's standards or guidelines. The magazine also reserves the right to remove or modify any content that is deemed inappropriate or offensive, at its sole discretion.

MAMA acknowledges and respects the rights of all individuals and groups and will not publish any content that promotes hate speech, discrimination, or any form of violence. The magazine also respects the privacy of its contributors and readers and will not share or sell any personal information to third parties without prior written consent.

By submitting their work to MAMA, the author agrees to abide by these copyright specifics and to grant the magazine the rights outlined in this statement. The author also certifies that their work is original and does not infringe on the rights of any third party. MAMA reserves the right to modify these copyright specifics at any time without prior notice.

If you have any questions or concerns regarding these copyright specifics, please contact MAMA at info@martialartsmagazineaustralia.com

An Ode to my Dad
by Ben Ward

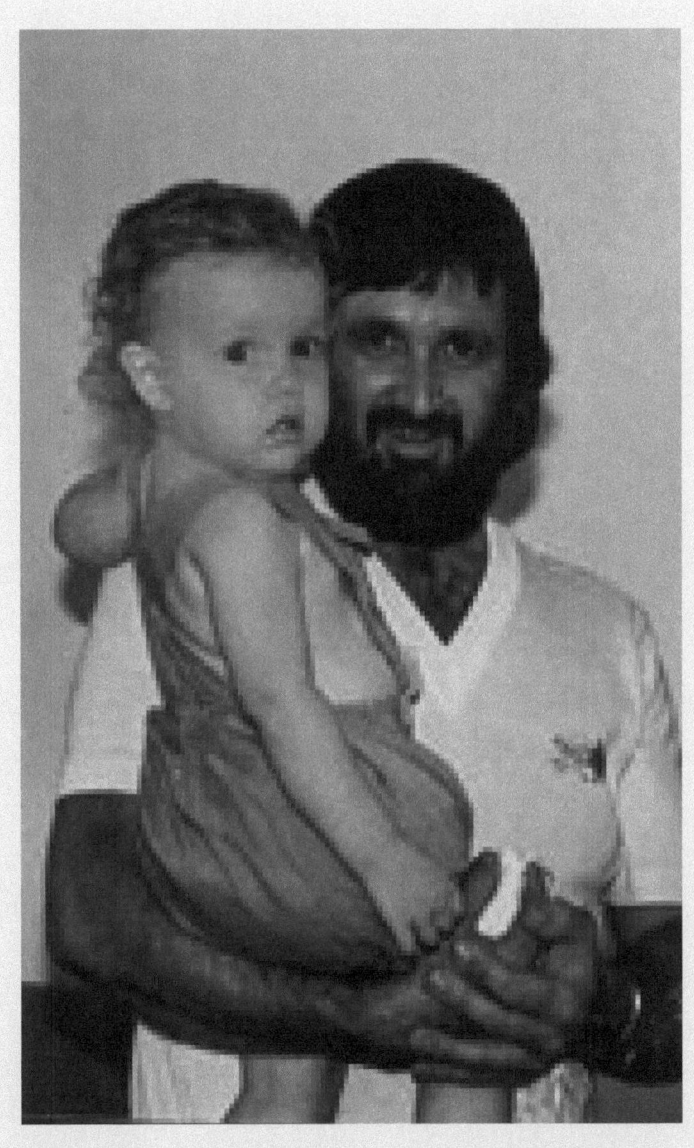

Most martial arts masters have a way to make a living outside of martial arts to avoid corruption of their values. These values were disregarded in my own martial arts style in the 80s. A style that I have done since I was thirteen.

I have only ever been a part of three other martial arts dojos in my life. One while I was in grades 4-6 with my mum, a traditional style. Then I was with Bob Jone's Zen Do Kai freestyle from the age of thirteen.

When I was fifteen, there was dissent in the power structure and the second in charge under Bob Jones', Kru Malcolm Anderson. Bob Jones started Zen Do Kai in the 1970s in Melbourne's inner suburbs as a style that incorporates the best of everything. It was an ethos similar to Bruce Lee's, but also a tradition that reaches as far back as the beginning of martial arts. Bob Jones would bail up Asian workers getting off the ships coming from overseas in the 70s and ask to learn their martial arts.

He incorporated this with the Goju Kai he had learned under Tino Ceberano; therefore, a lot of Zen Do Kai's katas are from Goju Kai and Ryu. He started a club in Melbourne and Malcolm Anderson ran his second club, having got his black belt under him.

Fast forward to the year 2001 and Malcolm decided Bob was only in it for the money and he separated from him to control all the clubs in Queensland and called it Zen Do Kai QLD.

We still had all the same BJC (Bob Jones corporation) grading sheets at our gradings we were just told to black out the logo (such as on my own black belt certificate).

Not all clubs went with Malcolm, and many clubs didn't want to be involved with the politics. Many clubs shut down never to open again, disheartened by the feuding and power plays. Six years later when I rejoined Zen Do Kai QLD, it had changed its name to Anderson Bushi Kai and perhaps because of the 'bushy' in the name, it was very popular in the bush/rural suburbs of QLD.

Our style now has a heritage of moving away from corruption at the highest levels to study more traditional martial arts practices. Our style has become much more traditional and many of the muay Thai kickboxing elements are not present in the karate classes as there is now a distinction between kickboxing clubs and classes in karate rather than the Zen do Kai freestyle which was a mix of muay Thai, karate, and wrestling arts - such as the now nonexistent shoot fighting of the 80s and 90s. Shoot fighting existed before the UFC and to shoot is to take someone down from standing and to remain standing yourself. Although, it included many finishing locks and moves from an advantage position on the ground. It was freestyle karate with an emphasis on takedowns to end a fight. You won't find a shoot fighting club anywhere in Australia now and they were rare to begin with.

The corruption of Zen Do Kai began with its inception. While my own instructors led me to believe the 'Jet Black system' was in the 80s, my Dad told me when I started Zen Do Kai that in the very early 70s (ITS BEGINNING) you could become a black belt in a year with Zen Do Kai. So, there were a lot of Zen Do Kai black belts running around in the 70s and 80s who couldn't fight. This is corrupt. As long as they paid the money, they got a belt.

My dad had two stories from when he was a teenager about Zen Do Kai black belts as he encountered them. The first goes as follows:

My dad was standing talking to an acquaintance he knew on a Brisbane street and coming up behind this fella was a guy who jumped out of a car and was going to king hit him from behind. My dad grabbed his acquaintance friend by the scruff of the neck and pulled him in close to himself as the ZDK black belt threw a haymaker from behind. This acquaintance thought my dad was the one king hit wrestling him and was trying to hurt him but then my dad let go of this guy and grabbed the black belt by his shirt and the back of his belt and threw him back into the open door of the car he jumped out of where he split open his head on the inside of the opposite door and they drove off. Now this acquaintance who was being attacked wasn't particularly my dad's friend, but my dad didn't believe in king hitters.

A couple of weeks later, my dad was looking in a shop window when he saw in the reflection someone jumping toward him from beside and behind him. He saw it was a flying sidekick, so he ducked. This was the same king hitter Zen Do Kai guy from weeks before. When you do a flying sidekick, you can't change direction midair. This guy flew over my dad's head and landed awkwardly on the ground beside him.

"Ow, ow, I think I've broken my ankle,"

To which my dad said, "You were going to kick me right?" He kicked the guy in the face and left.

Now you think that would have been the end of it.

Weeks later, 'Frostie' had a party and Bob Jones was providing security for it. He was pretty famous at this time and was on TV doing self-defense for women, etc. Everyone knew Bob Jones was going to be there. When my dad saw Bob Jones, he said he was a very tall guy with very wide shoulders and built like a brick dunny so no one was going to mess with him anyway. My dad was pretty short by comparison but built like a rugby player and had benched 100kg around this time. As well as a year in boxing. My dad was at the party with my mum, his later to be wife of 50 years, but at this point they were just boyfriend and girlfriend. While he was there, this guy that he had kicked in the face was there with two other friends and they went up to Bob Jones and whined that is the guy who beat me up. So Bob Jones walks toward my dad and my dad doesn't know what to expect, so he moves his back to the wall as Bob comes up to speak with him.

So, you see, in my own household, Zen Do Kai didn't stand for much at all. And my dad wanted me to go back to a traditional style. In the end Malcolm Anderson has turned ABK freestyle karate into a much more traditional style and belts aren't given out as readily but it still happened in the Zen Do Kai of the 90s as I was disqualified for making contact with a girl who cried her eyes out and then won the tournament. Hmm, my dad always remembered that one. Like if you can't take a hit, then you shouldn't practice martial arts. We were teenagers and it was an accident.

Many laughs were shared in our high caliber dojo, but the politicians ran the tournaments for sure. I later sparred an older lady in her late 20s when I was just 16 and she was dating a 28-year-old 5th Dan who was a 2nd dan in shoot fighting. I did a spinning back kick in haste to rise to the occasion, and she did a sidekick at exactly the same time with the same speed. Well, I ended up with sore nuts and her boyfriend taught me to jump up in the air and land on my heels to remove the effect. It worked effectively, amazingly and immediately. Well, of course, I went around jumping and landing on my heels for the rest of the day and explaining this neat trick to all my classmates. That was a good day.

Just last year I tried my third dojo. This club was five minutes from my home, and I thought I could save money from the twenty-minute drive to my old club. I joined; it didn't work out. The instructor used my giri as an excuse to trick me into tearing my ACL by teaching me to do kicks as fast as I could from a parallel stance with no pivoting allowed. After I tore my hamstring that day doing the exercise, I left the club, but I had made lifelong acquaintances among the other white belt students.

And so, I've returned to my old club in Coolum and was welcomed back on a barometer of effort put in and respect will be earned. I learned immediately that the club's ethos of being a good person has become paramount since I left and ventured into a scary world where I've avoided conflict by following what my dad said about being a black belt. To avoid a fight, just don't be there. My instructor has said this too, and there are many parallels between my instructor and my father.

The lightbulb moment was that the club ethos of being a good person was paramount when I trained there in my 20s and I can see it is a standard that is upheld by other father figures and mentors and like the crazy uncles that are there too, and I see why in Chinese gong fu they call each other brothers and sisters and teacher too.

Both my instructors and my dad pushed me to work in paid employment when I was in my 20s and training and I did for the next nine years as a pamphlet deliverer, filter exchange specialist, cleaner, removalist, barman, and a stock assistant. It is only now that I know my inner self hasn't been corrupted by the politics of my karate style in the past and the many wolves in sheep's clothing I have met and never knew it. All because of my commitment to martial arts.

And on this day, the day that my dad has passed away I am so glad I was born into a fighter's family and I am happy for my martial arts family and I realise martial arts will always be a way for me to connect with others through something I love doing, and I will never truly EVER be alone.

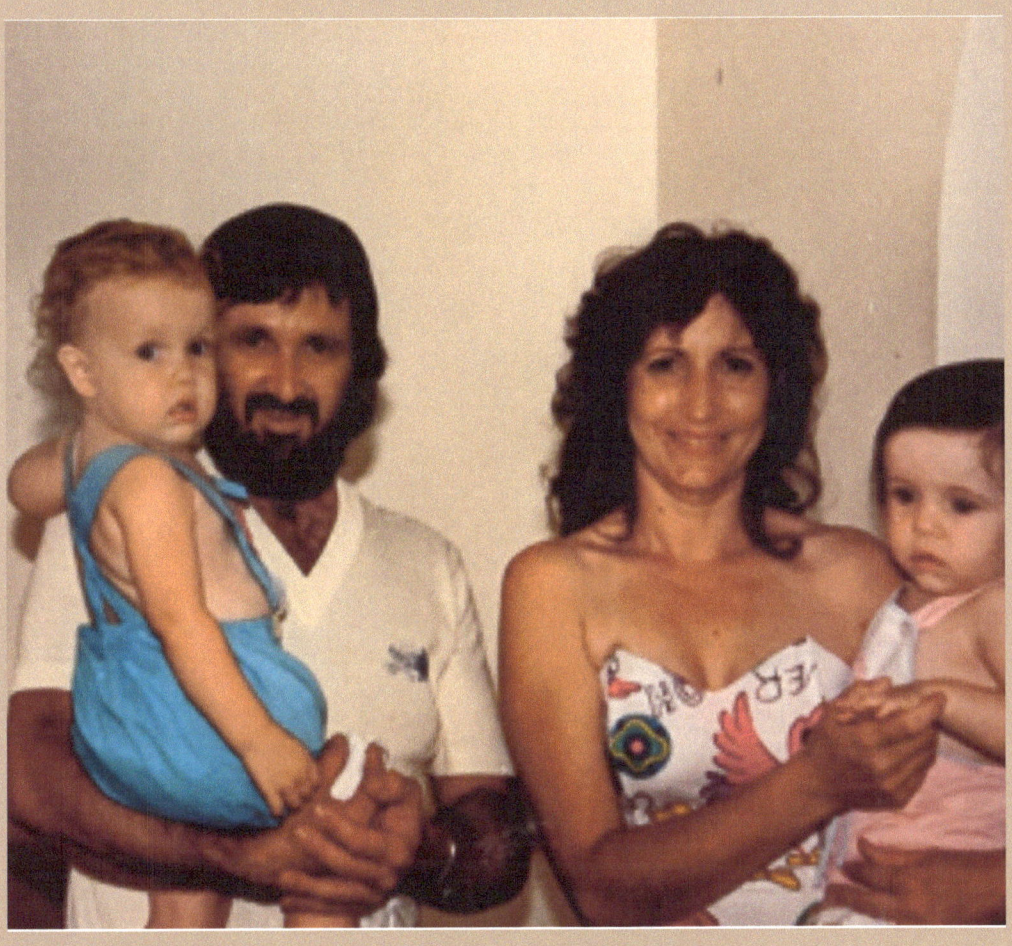

Pictured: Ben Ward, Kevin Ward and Colleen Ward.

Christianne Blenkin

Finding her way back to Jiujitsu After Stepping off the mat for 10 Years

Image & article by Sheryl Sumugat

Christianne Blenkin is the first and currently, the only female brown belt of Toowoomba's Behan Jiujitsu gym. Like a lot of women today, she wears different hats: doting wife, mum of two, yogi, BJJ kids' coach, and an actively training and competing Jiujiteira. Just this year, she's already competed twice, and took three gold medals, one silver, and two overall trophies for women's gi and no gi.

I invited her for an interview to chat about her Jiujitsu journey. As a female white belt who trains at the same gym as her, her persistence and tenacity are a source of inspiration. I was compelled to know more of her story when I learned that she has been training for 20 years, but with a 10-year break. The story about what made her leave and what pushed her to come back is something I believe women in martial arts could learn a lot from.

Q: How did you discover Jiujitsu and what made you give it a go? It was when I was in my 20's and I was kind of a little bit lost. I used to train at the gym, but I used to watch the Jiujitsu class. It was a big gym, and the Jiujitsu class was the last class of the day. I never actually stayed till the end of Jiujitsu but what I used to watch was the warm-ups, so I would see them doing forward rolls and backward rolls, cartwheels, and I was a gymnast, so I was like "Oh this looks fun. I would be good at it". The coach kept saying, "You should come and give it a try." So, I gave it a try.

I come from a background of alcohol and drug addiction, so I used Jiujitsu as my new thing. All my focus and energy went into Jiujitsu so that my life didn't go into addiction, spiraling downwards. So, I entered it with such ferocity. I started competing immediately and not just locally. I went internationally, nationally, and just pushed and pushed and pushed until my body was broken. And then they said, you might not have kids if you don't stop.
Life was hard and painful. Jiujitsu was a thing that I would use each day to pick myself up.

Q: So why did you stop?
I pushed myself so hard that I lost my love for it. I had retired and then I just decided to go to Pans Pacific just to see how I went in 2010. When I got down there, I got paired with the brown and the black belt. I was a purple belt, and I won the division. And then, I had people interested in sending me to the Worlds. So, I went to the Worlds and I was teaching females at the time as well. I took one of my students over at the Worlds. When I got there, I realized I've made a huge mistake. I didn't have the fight in me anymore. Also, because I've been told "Oh your body's broken." I was told, "Don't go down the weight division, because your body can't handle it", so I tried to go upper weight division, but my body wouldn't take on the extra weight. By the time I got over there, I had fallen back into the division below and then I was fighting big monsters.
After I went to the Worlds, I never went back to Jiujitsu again.

Q: Could you tell us why?
I think I felt like that chapter was done. I pushed and pushed, and I was doing it because I was good at it, not because I loved it. And then when I got over there, I realized that if you don't love it, then you can't push yourself to do it. So, I came home, and I didn't say goodbye to my coach. I just left.

Q: How did you get back to it?
Well, over the years, my husband has always encouraged it. We got together just as my Jiujitsu journey ended, but he knew me before, so he knew my Jiujitsu journey. "You should go back," but I was like, "I'm done!" I started doing yoga to heal my body and my mind. I felt like I had a lot of stuff that I needed to process. Jiujitsu became more like an outlet for my anger. Eventually, when my son was looking for a sport, we've tried everything, but he just didn't like anything, and I thought, "You know what he's a lot like me, I bet he'd like Jiujitsu." And I took him to a class, and he loved it. I was like, this is what he was meant to be doing because we have similar personalities. It didn't take long. I was watching and then my body knew the movements, and my body just wanted to be on the mats. I resisted for a little while.

Q: Why did you resist?
Because it's a confusing journey. There's so many ups and downs in your Jiujitsu journey, like in line with your life. And I've just yoga'd myself calm and they're like the yin and the yang. They're opposite but they're aligned.

Q: Like they complement each other.
Yes. And I believe that I'm a way better fighter now that I've got a yoga background. Way calmer, less ego, and more about embracing the fun and the connection, finding the safe space where you can be a mess, knowing that your teammates have your back.

Q: What were your biggest struggles and how did you overcome them?
Being a woman in the sport that many years ago. I was the only woman in the class, so finding fair fights, I thought, was a balance of being patronized because they dont wanna hurt you or being too rough because they didn't wanna be beaten by a girl. I found it really hard, and also being able to figure out where you sit on the scale when you don't have any women to fight against. That was the reason I travelled a lot, because I wanted to see what my
capabilities were against other women. I had to go where the girls were. I was going where I could find competition. I was very competitive.

Q: What would be your advice to women like me who struggle with the motivation to train, and turning off their motherly, gentle side?
Find your people that you're safe with. Communicate with them what you need. Advocate for yourself. Be really honest. When you're rolling, if somebody's done something that you don't like, tell them— which is really scary because there's that fear

of judgement. But I feel like you will have more honest and safe rolls if you can be really, really open. Like it's okay to say, "That was really rough". And the best rolls I had were with the people where we check in with each other constantly.

Q: How would you define too rough in JiuJitsu?

It totally depends on where you're heads at at that moment in time, which is why it is something that you constantly need to express. What you thought was rough yesterday is totally different from what you think is rough today, depending on what's going on with your life. So, you have to feel like these people that you're rolling with understand that. And I totally find those people in the gym. Some people feel their feelings in the mat. So, if they come in and they had a bad day, they're gonna tear your limbs off, because that's the way that they could express it. You just gotta be aware of other people's energy and you have to be okay to say, "Not today" to people. It's okay when you first start to have a small circle of people you feel safe with, and then when you feel safe and ready, slowly move out of your circle. Even as a high-ranking belt, I still do that. I don't rush into being like I should be able to roll with all these different people, because that's what it's all about. You've gotta nurture your own growth.

Q: Lastly, do you believe that a Jiujitsu gym is a place for women, and how do women affect its culture?

I absolutely think that women belong in the gym, especially as a kids coach. I think it's really important to show the next generation that women are warriors too. Having female coaches for the kids' class is amazing, because boys get to go, "Oh, women are strong!" and not just having that pure male presence. I think that women need support from other women in a place like that to know that they do belong. People like me are a pinnacle in seeing that your journey can continue over the years, through motherhood, through so many changes, that in can still be there, and that it can still be something you can benefit from. We kinda offer a softness, maybe, a balance. We offer the yin and the yang energy. Men would find rolling with women different. I think that will help their game, because we're more technical. We fight differently. We bring technique.

Image by Miljan Zivovic

"An injury is not just a process of recovery. It's a process of discovery."
— Connor McGregor

Recovery to Discovery
10 Tips to continue training when injured
by Peter Zarb

Injuries happen, and often at the most inconvenient times. It's Murphy's Law.

Ages ago, I can't remember the year, I had an industrial accident resulting in a tuft fracture and half of my thumb less attached than is normal. The plastic surgeon did an excellent job knitting it all back together - I mean it was impressive.

I was genuinely surprised by how much I was encouraged to return to work as soon as able, and my regular duties were modified to suit my [dis]ability. It turns out, each state has a 'return to work' policy aimed at supporting injured workers to get back into a normal routine. Why? Studies show it aids physical and mental recovery, and helps maintain skill levels.

When injured, people are far more likely to be sedentary when at home compared to going to your work, school or enjoying extra-curricular activities. Plus. The isolation and impotence of being stuck at home all day with an injury can cause poor mental health, especially if you have been an active individual.

You also start losing skills as soon as you stop practising them. While it may never go away completely, the longer the period between practicing or doing, the harder it is to pick up where you left off.

Then there is the social support you get from returning to normal activities. People often think of family and friends as their support network, but colleagues, teammates and training buddies can play equally important roles.

I saw the value of this first-hand (pun intended) so I integrated the same principles and strategies into my own training and teaching. The week following my injury, I was back in the dojo demonstrating single-handed self-defence tactics.

> "We cannot choose our external circumstances, but we can always choose how we respond to them."
> — Epictetus

We cannot avoid injuries our whole lives – I mean on a long enough timeline, right. Interestingly, this article wasn't originally written with the above story in mind. In the last 3-year period, I personally know 15+ young people and 1 adult who have suffered fall and impact-based injuries that include broken arms, vertebrae, legs, wrists, toe and a hip! 2 were karateka and, no, it didn't happen in the dojo.

This article was inspired to help these community members bounce back from their injuries and stay well physically and mentally.

Here are my 10 tips to getting back to training while injured and in recovery.

1. Listen to your medical professionals (not DR Google)

Specialists train very hard. It would be counter-productive to ignore a professional's advice. Surgeons, doctors, nurses, physiotherapists: hear them out. They want what is best for you. Don't get me wrong. I'm all about getting second and third opinions and making sure the advice I'm given is consistent and right for me. Some professionals are specialised in certain fields, for example, the hand therapist who helped with the rehabilitation on my thumb. A general practitioner, while a capable medical professional, may not have the specialised knowledge that my hand therapist or orthopaedic surgeon had. That's where referrals come in. Get the right advice. Then stick to it.

2. Read

Whatever your passion is - karate, rugby, competitive rock, paper, scissors – find books, blogs and articles, and do some research. What are its origins, history, influences and key influencers? How has it developed over time? Etc. Exercise your mind - it is one of your most important organs after all. Remember, knowledge is power.

"To truly master karate-do one must embody the entire philosophy; without a strong and virtuous mind, the body is useless."
– *Ohtsuka Tadahiko Sensei, Goju Kensha Saishinkan Japan*

3. Watch: Classes/sessions.

You'll be surprised what you can pick up from simply watching others train. How people move, their posture and technique. You are looking for what is being done correctly or different and comparing it to how you do it. I'm not talking about being judgmental: simply observing. Listen intently to the coach give students advice or correction. This guidance could also apply to you. A word to the wise – don't give unsolicited advice (says the guy writing the article). Some people don't know they need help, or they don't want it. You do you.

4. Watch: YouTube/Instagram/Vimeo, etc.

You will need to filter. Flashy introductions are not necessarily an accurate representation of quality. There is danger with inexperienced people picking up bad habits from poor quality resources. There are some amazing diamonds amid the hundreds of thousands of videos online. Sadly, there is also quite a lot of questionable content and coaches. If you are an experienced athlete in your selected art/activity, then this filtering process will be swift. If not, ask your coach for direction to appropriate supplementary material for you.

"Katatsumuri, soro soro nobore, fuji no yama"
"O snail, Climb Mt. Fuji, But slowly, slowly!"

— Kobayashi Issa (小林一茶)

5. Go slow

Excitedly rushing into training can cause more injury. I remember arriving at the dojo after having a suspected melanoma removed; three stitches. It was all going well until I got a little too eager, BAM went the punch and POP went two stitches.

It is ok to go slow. In fact, I'd argue that going slow is essential for developing the appropriate technique.

You create the correct neural pathways and muscular control by deliberately practicing slowly. If you can do it slow perfectly, you can do it fast perfectly.

Don't think that you can hide poor technique in speed from an experienced instructor *wink*. The military use the saying "slow is smooth and smooth is fast".

6. Work with what you have… left

Hurt a leg, you've still got two arms and a leg. Hurt an arm and you've two legs and an arm. Basically, work with what you have that still functions, providing that it does not cause referred discomfort. Listen to your body. Never push through a trauma-based pain. If it is hurting, do not do it.

Experience and intelligence mixed with determination is the perfect formula for innovation. If you have a skilled and qualified trainer, they will be able to innovate and demonstrate exercises and strategies that enable you to train risk free. This is the hallmark of a true master of their craft.

7. Immobilise the injury

You can't be trusted: trust me. Those reflexes you've spent hours honing - they're dangerous. If you immobilise the injury, you reduce the risk of an automated, unconscious response that could exacerbate your injury. Wrap it, strap it, and be cautious. It is your body and your responsibility to ensure you have it in great working order for life.

You create the correct neural pathways and muscular control by deliberately practicing slowly. If you can do it slow perfectly, you can do it fast perfectly.

Don't think that you can hide poor technique in speed from an experienced instructor *wink*. The military use the saying "slow is smooth and smooth is fast".

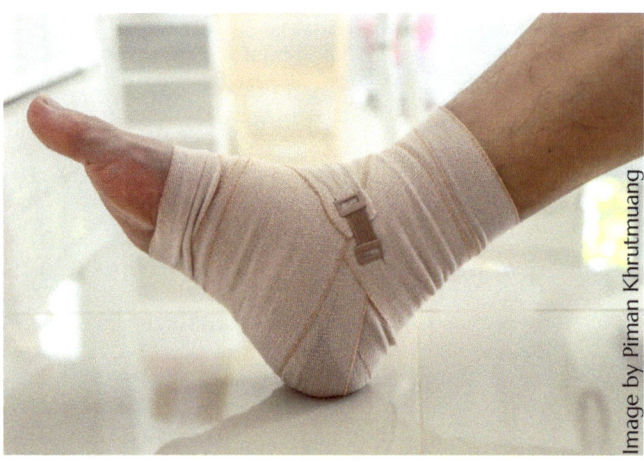

8. Basics

These are the fundamentals of your training. They are essential and, in most cases, can be practiced independently. These skills are important to keep up so long as they do not cause you pain. Dribbling a ball, kicking a footy, punching and kicking; do what you can to keep active, slowly and carefully.

9. Pair and group activities

Avoid spontaneity. Only through carefully planned activities can you hope to train alongside others without injury. Your goal should be risk-free training in a safe, supportive environment.

Do not compete, period. We are hard-wired for survival. The sympathetic nervous system responses can create the right biochemical results to do well in the moment, but after will leave you in a much worse position than when you started. Keep things simple and structured. One on one is ok but adding more people to the mix creates unnecessary complexity.

10. It is ok to not be ok

Having an injury can be hard work, physically and emotionally. Reach out to your coach and team-mates. This could be as simple as starting a small conversation about training methods or as huge as confiding how you are feeling. There are great bonds of friendship that develop within genuine health and wellbeing communities - fighting arts especially. There is a level of trust that can transcend everyday friendships; I am putting my physical wellbeing in your hands, or rather fists, after all. These people will want to help, even if it is to lend you an ear to hear or a shoulder to cry on. Showing emotion is never a weakness, in fact it is our greatest strength - acknowledging our vulnerability rather than pretending to be invincible.

With the right mindset, an injury has the potential to reveal some great things about you. As Seneca the Younger said, **"A gem cannot be polished without friction, nor a person perfected without trials."**

About Peter Zarb

6th dan Goju [Kensha] Ryu Karate black belt. Peter Zarb, is described by fellow karate experts as:
"A thinking gentleman warrior - highly trained, unassuming, accommodating and friendly. It is rare to find people of the younger generation who are as knowledgeable about true martial arts as Pete."

Peter's training under renowned masters in Australia, Japan and Taiwan has helped mould him into the natural and skilled instructor he is today. He has been studying karate since he was a young boy and teaching for over 20 years. Peter has spent decades researching and supplementing his training experience with complimentary and influential combat arts, including other karate style, judo, and internal kung fu. He is a generous, outgoing and knowledgeable instructor whose humorous, easy going attitude spreads throughout the dojo. But do not be fooled, you will train very hard with him.

The Art of Being a Role Model
Inspiration & Leadership in Martial Arts

by Maria Francis

In the world of martial arts, the concept of a role model extends far beyond mere skill or technique. It encompasses a holistic approach to life, embodying principles that shape not just martial artists, but well-rounded individuals.

Being a role model in martial arts is about more than executing perfect kicks or winning tournaments. It's about embodying the core values of martial arts in every aspect of life. A true role model demonstrates respect, discipline, integrity, and perseverance both on and off the mat.

Take, for instance, the story of Sarah Thompson, a 35-year-old karate instructor from Melbourne. Despite facing a debilitating car accident that left her with chronic pain, Sarah continued to teach and practice, showing her students that true strength comes from within. "I could have given up," Sarah says, "but I realised that my struggles could inspire others to push through their own challenges."

A role model in martial arts sets an example not just in physical prowess, but in mental and emotional resilience. They show that martial arts is a way of life, not just a sport or hobby.

Rules to Live By

To be an effective role model in a martial arts school, one must adhere to certain rules:

1. Practice What You Preach: Consistency between words and actions is crucial. If you emphasise the importance of discipline, you must demonstrate it in your own life.

2. Continuous Learning: A good role model never stops being a student. They remain humble and open to learning, even from those junior to them.

3. Respect for All: Treat everyone with equal respect, regardless of their rank, age, or background.

4. Ethical Behaviour: Uphold high ethical standards both in and out of the dojo.

5. Emotional Control: Demonstrate the ability to manage emotions, especially in challenging situations.

6. Community Involvement: Engage in community service and encourage students to do the same.

7. Healthy Lifestyle: Maintain a balanced, healthy lifestyle that reflects the principles of martial arts.

8. Honesty and Integrity: Always be truthful and act with integrity, even when it's difficult.

9. Perseverance: Show resilience in the face of setbacks and challenges.

10. Empathy and Compassion: Understand and relate to the struggles of others, offering support and guidance.

Danny, a TKD isntructor from Armadale, exemplifies these rules in his daily life. Known for his community outreach programs, John uses martial arts to help at-risk youth. "Living by these rules isn't always easy," John admits, "but it's necessary if we want to make a real difference in people's lives."

Qualities to Portray

A role model in martial arts should embody several key qualities:

Qualities to Portray

A role model in martial arts should embody several key qualities:

1. Humility: Despite their skills and achievements, a good role model remains humble and grounded.

2. Patience: They show patience with students of all levels, understanding that everyone learns at their own pace.

3. Passion: Their love for martial arts is evident in everything they do, inspiring others to develop the same passion.

4. Resilience: They demonstrate the ability to bounce back from failures and setbacks.

5. Leadership: They lead by example, taking initiative and guiding others with wisdom and compassion.

6. Adaptability: They show flexibility in their teaching methods, adapting to different learning styles and situations.

7. Self-discipline: They exhibit strong self-control and dedication to their practice.

8. Empowerment: They focus on building others up, helping students discover their own strengths and potential.

9. Authenticity: They remain true to themselves and their values, even in the face of pressure or adversity.

10. Continuous improvement: They constantly strive to better themselves, both in martial arts and in life.

Inspiring others to become role models themselves is a crucial aspect of leadership in martial arts. Here are some strategies to encourage this:

1. Lead by Example: The most powerful way to inspire others is through your own actions. Consistently demonstrate the qualities and behaviours you wish to see in others.

2. Recognise and Reward Positive Behaviour: Acknowledge students who exhibit role model qualities. This could be through verbal praise, special responsibilities, or formal recognition.

3. Create Mentorship Programs: Pair senior students with juniors, giving them the opportunity to develop leadership skills and become role models themselves.

4. Discuss the Importance of Being a Role Model: Incorporate talks about character development and the responsibility of being a role model into your regular classes.

5. Provide Opportunities for Growth: Offer leadership roles and community service opportunities to students, allowing them to practice being role models.

6. Share Stories of Inspiring Figures: Use examples from martial arts history and current events to illustrate what it means to be a role model.

7. Encourage Reflection: Promote self-awareness by encouraging students to reflect on their actions and how they impact others.

8. Set Clear Expectations: Clearly communicate the standards of behavior expected in and out of the dojo.

9. Address Mistakes Constructively: When students fall short, use it as a learning opportunity rather than just a moment for punishment.

10. Celebrate Progress: Recognise not just achievements, but also effort and improvement in becoming a better role model.

Being a role model isn't without its challenges. It's important to acknowledge and address these potential pitfalls:

1. Pressure of Perfection: Role models might feel pressured to appear perfect at all times. It's crucial to remember that showing vulnerability and how to handle mistakes is also part of being a good role model.

2. Burnout: The responsibility of being a constant example can be exhausting. Self-care and maintaining a healthy work-life balance are essential.

3. Resistance from Others: Not everyone may appreciate or understand the high standards you're trying to uphold. Patience and perseverance are key in these situations.

4. Balancing Authority and Approachability: As a role model, you need to maintain a level of authority while still being approachable and relatable to your students.

5. Handling Fame or Recognition: If you achieve some level of fame or recognition, staying grounded and true to your values can become more challenging.

Mark Johnson, a Kung Fu instructor from Sydney, shares his experience: "There were times when I felt overwhelmed by the expectation to always be 'on.' I had to learn that being a role model doesn't mean being perfect; it means being authentic and showing others how to navigate life's challenges with grace and integrity."

The impact of being a good role model in martial arts extends far beyond the dojo. Students who are inspired by positive role models often carry these lessons into their personal and professional lives, creating a ripple effect of positive influence.

Lisa Chen, a corporate executive and longtime Aikido practitioner, credits her martial arts training and the example set by her sensei for her leadership style. "The principles I learned in the dojo – respect, perseverance, and continuous improvement – have been invaluable in my career," Lisa says. "I try to embody these same principles as a leader in my company."

This ripple effect can have far-reaching consequences. When martial arts students become role models in their own spheres of influence – be it in their families, schools, or workplaces – they spread the core values of martial arts to a wider audience, contributing to a more respectful, disciplined, and harmonious society.

Being a role model in a martial arts school is a profound responsibility and a continuous journey of self-improvement. It requires living by a strict code of ethics, portraying admirable qualities, and consistently inspiring others to reach their full potential.

The essence of being a martial arts role model lies not in perfection, but in the sincere effort to embody the principles of martial arts in daily life. It's about showing others that the true power of martial arts lies not just in physical techniques, but in its ability to forge strong character and positive values.

As martial artists strive to be role models, they not only elevate themselves but also uplift their students and communities. They become living examples of the transformative power of martial arts, inspiring others to embark on their own journeys of self-discovery and personal growth.

In the words of the legendary Bruce Lee, "Knowledge will give you power, but character respect." As role models in martial arts, we have the opportunity and the responsibility to build both knowledge and character – in ourselves and in others. By doing so, we honour the true spirit of martial arts and contribute to creating a more respectful, disciplined, and compassionate world.

Role model: noun "a person looked to by others as an example to be imitated." (google)

The Interview
by Attila Halasz

Welcome to my third story in this magazine.

Apparently it is hot in Budapest at the end of August.

I took public transportation to the large sports centre on the outskirts.

Being 1996 and no mobile phones and widely available internet, all I knew about aikido grandmaster Yasuo Kobayashi that he was 50 years old and an 8th dan aikido black belt.

He started training in 1955 and was a direct student of the founder, Morihei Ueshiba and the great, Koichi Tohei. He spent 10 years training with the latter, Tohei was also my own teacher's major influence.

When I walked through the grounds, there was a leafy, outdoor area littered with a great number of participants. I was looking for Kobayashi Shihan with great excitement. I imagined a towering personality, surrounded by his own black belts, and I thought, as a very important teacher, he'd be wearing a fine business suit with a tie.

I suddenly noticed a larger than normal gathering around a table. I could hear someone laughing. The man sitting and laughing, looked Japanese and fifty. He wore a green bucket hat, a yellow T-shirt and green cargo pants with brown sandals on his bare feet..
That somewhat eccentrically dressed person can't be Kobayashi! - I thought to myself, but it was him!

Chatting in English, relaxed and casual, he was charming, friendly and accessible.
In comparison, I've seen plenty of pompous teachers on my European aikido journey.

Later the training hall was totally packed with international aikido students from all over. I stopped counting at one hundred.

Every young black belt's dream is to get closer to the grandmaster but in this massive crowd I resigned myself to the fact that I'll just have to watch him from the back.

But that afternoon, during the wooden staff training class, an unexpected opportunity presented itself!

Kobayashi was showing various techniques on what happens when someone would grab and take the jo (staff) from him. However, during these advanced techniques, his ukes just couldn't take proper, safe falls when thrown fast and dynamically by him.

Seeing that, I quickly moved forward to the front row. Kobayashi, as so far he couldn't bring his point across, looked around for another, hopefully better uke. When our eyes locked, I bowed to him quickly.

He signaled for me to go out. I grabbed his jo strongly and he threw me fast and hard. I was back up immediately and ready to go again!
I wasn't fazed, even when he swept my feet from under me with the hard wooden stick. He was indeed satisfied at the end of the demo.

From then on, I sat in the first row, always close and paying attention.

Every time when his uke didn't respond the way it was expected for the demo, he glanced at me and I was up and ready. For five days, I assisted him continuously.

I thought back to my white belt years (Shin Sen Dojo in Sydney) taking so much ukemi. I really didn't like it at the beginning as throwing people was much more fun than being thrown, but master Ken was right. I had the time of my life in Budapest now.

The skin came off my toes and my entire body was hurting but it was kind of a beautiful and worthwhile feeling.

During the nights I slept on the mats on the dojo floor like many others and coffee never tasted better than at 6 am at the nearby petrol station.

In the following days, I became a popular figure at this seminar because of my daring falls. I made many new friends. During a break, Kobayashi shihan asked me if I was going to stay in Europe and join his organisation! I couldn't hide my happiness... and my sadness as my travels were coming to an end and I had to leave.

Everyone would get tired after a five day long intensive.

I clearly saw that Kobayashi was also tired and I was spent too.

After the last class I walked up to him:
I have been practicing Ki Shiatsu massage...if you'd like one- I said to the grandmaster. He responded with a big smile.
I've done many massages over the years but I really tried my best now.

I really thought that my aikido learning finished for the day but it wasn't so.

To my great surprise, the relaxed and elegantly throwing Kobayashi had a massive back, forged like steel. His arms and legs were like iron too! He had powerful muscles and the long decades of hard training were clearly showing. He was massively strong!

There was much talk in the aikido community about being gentle and smooth but I also read in a martial arts magazine that Ueshiba's disciples were strong and powerful. It was so astonishing to confirm that now!

Kobayashi sat up refreshed after the massage. He complimented my effort. I was over the moon.

What would you like to ask? - he turned to me as we sat together.

During our lunch break earlier I enquired if I could ask him about aikido founder Morihei Ueshiba who died in 1969. My only chance!

I took a big breath and I was ready. At that moment I saw a local TV crew arriving with camera and microphone, ready for an official interview but Kobayashi didn't look at them at all.

Even more humbled now, I asked about the old ways of training, the so-called "secret techniques" and other masters like Koichi Tohei and what Ueshiba was like as a day to day person.

I also asked him about his own relationship with the founder of aikido.

Hahaha...he liked me, especially because I made him laugh- Kobayashi remembered the old days with a smile.

There was one more question I originally didn't want to ask…but now I had to.

How come you were so informal and nice to us and not strict at all during this intensive?- I asked. I thought Japanese etiquette was tough?

Kobayashi laughed again.

"We are not in Japan. When I'm back home, there is a very strict code for me indeed. But aikido is for the world and for people to love it everywhere, we have to consider where we are." he added. It was the most inspiring conversation.

Other than the five magnificent days training intensely with the amazing Yasuo Kobayashi, there was one other moment I will never forget.

On the last day of training, I suddenly came face to face with a somewhat skinny person with black hair.

The moment he gripped my arm I felt that he was a black belt to reckon with! Not only couldn't I throw him, but as the star assistant to Kobayashi, I couldn't even move. He was incredibly powerful! His name was Robert and he was from the Nakajima group, Germany.

Never mind me…or this situation. Mind that if I am able to stop you then someone else will stop you too, or worse a real person of danger…- he said before changing partners and he disappeared in the crowds. I took note. Decided to train even harder and made the promise to myself to become mighty and unstoppable.

Two weeks later, my flight took off from Vienna. After a year in Europe I was heading home to Sydney. I was so excited to see master Ken and my fellow student friends at our Paddlington dojo! I couldn't wait to share everything that I learned and experienced in Europe.

Unknown to me and all of us in the dojo that soon a devastating shadow, the ultimate foe, death itself will pay a visit to our community. Unfairly and so brutally would take a life that would leave all of us speechless and in tears. The grief will be felt for years. I had to realise then, that no amount of training or black belts will save me when it comes to my last stand facing death. Ultimately we all will be alone at the gate.

I cried and you will too. But that's another story to tell.

My Martial Art Influencers
by Chris McVay

Many years ago, when I was 13 years old, at school I was a pretty outgoing kid with a few friends doing all sorts of stuff.

As a kid I did judo but nothing stuck, I was only six years old. When I was 13, I ran into a bit of trouble and was surrounded by thugs who took it upon themselves to use my head as a punching bag. They left me for dead in the street with permanent damage.

When I was young, I loved the action and martial arts movies along with sci-fi. I got influenced by my first movie star, Jean Claude Van Damme. I loved the kickboxing style, then I found more great martial arts movies. I watch Cynthia Rothrock, Michael Dudikoff, Bruce lee, Chuck Norris, Sammo Hung and Jackie Chan. I can safely say they all influenced me to start my martial arts journey.

I think Van Damme, being a bit of a poser, started me on the splits training. (picture of me doing the van dam splits over two chairs in tui glen campsite NZ). I found a place in the UK to train at 13. I started with ninjutsu. My teacher, John Aitkin was training under Brian McCarthy and Masaaki Hatsumi so he was good and it was genuine training.

After a few years I moved to kickboxing for a while to follow my Van Damme showboating stuff in order to do the high kicks and splits, then moved away. Still with many influences I pursued my training with different instructors.

In the meantime, Facebook was introduced to the world, and many people were on it. I caught up with one of my idols and was only speaking recently. Cynthia Rothrock was on Facebook chatting to me, giving me positive feedback and letting me know about her upcoming movie. This was great, interaction with an idol at last. I told her the usual, which she has probably heard a million times, but she was happy and nice to chat to. Now at least I know, in life, no one is too good to talk to, and no one is better than anyone else. We are all equal in life even if we feel we are not. Just stop and help.

My favourite saying is, "each stranger is just a new friend you don't quite know yet." I live by that now and always look forward to chatting with fellow martial artists. I am currently training in Aikido. I am known as Aikido Chris and I assist in teaching people who need a bit of guidance and I help where I can in the dojo.

If I were to say who influences me now. I would definitively say my instructor Dave Mathews and my old Ninjutsu instructor in UK John Aitkin. They always have positive things to say and do to help with anything. See you at Port Kennedy Aikido.

> Martial Arts training is never easy, but you shouldn't give up. You'll get stronger and stay in shape, and one day the training may save your life.
>
> -Cynthia Rothrock

Australia's Hidden Wing Chun Legacy
by David Richardson

In this series of articles, I will recount some of the lessons and stories that have been shared with me during my training, and also over many Yum Cha with my Sifu, Gregory Choi, where we discuss many things relating to Wing Chun and Wing Chun Ling Tung Gong in particular.

I'll begin with a brief history of how Grandmaster Choi started Wing Chun under the legendary Wing Chun Grandmaster Yip Man and the knowledge of Wing Chun Ling Tung Gong that was passed down to him.

Grandmaster Gregory Choi (Tsoi Siu Kwong) began his training with Wing Chun Great Grand Master 葉問 Ip Man in 1954 at 東莞新街 Dong Goon San Gaai. Yip man had only been in that location for a short time after moving the club from 飯店公會 (Restaurant workers union). The name of the street was later changed to 利達街 Lei Dat Gaai which is how it is now famously remembered as the place that Bruce Lee first came to learn Wing Chun.

Yip Man taught in a traditional way and gave each student what they needed based on the individual's nature and also the strengths and weaknesses of the disciple. Just like in today's modern Wing Chun schools, there were different levels to the clubs student base. Most paid the standard fee of $30/month and as such were taught in the group class environment with the older students (Sihings) doing most of the teaching. Private lessons were given by Yip Man but there was no set fee. You gave him a red packet with what you could afford to pay. While it is true that the amount given to him was then reflected in what you were taught, it didn't guarantee that you would learn everything. There were many other factors that Yip Man took into account when accepting and teaching students.

Some students from this time period were taught how to use the martial aspect of Wing Chun over the internal aspect. This was because they showed interest and ability in this field and they would be good candidates to promote Yip Man's school and the efficiency of Wing Chun in challenge matches. GM Choi was not interested so much in proving himself in these challenge matches, however, he would spend every afternoon/evening and weekend training at the Lei Dat St club. Yip Man saw this talent & unbridled enthusiasm for Wing Chun in the young Master Choi and shared with him 4 books to copy detailing the art of Wing Chun Kuen , Wing Chun Ling Tung Gong & also Dit Da Medicine.

Sifu & Ipman

Sifu & Ipman

These books were written in 古文 Gu Man which is Classical Chinese prose or poems. And as it was, Grandmaster Choi's early years of schooling happened to be in a school that taught the old style of Gu Man 古文. This gave Sifu Choi the knowledge to not only read the text contained in the book but also be able to understand it's context & meanings to further develop the Ling Tung Gong system.

Without this understanding and early guidance from Yip Man it would've been easy to misinterpret some of the words and meanings which would change the outcome and understanding. And with the knowledge contained within these books, GM Choi has continued to develop the Qi Gong of Wing Chun Ling Tung Gong into its current form.

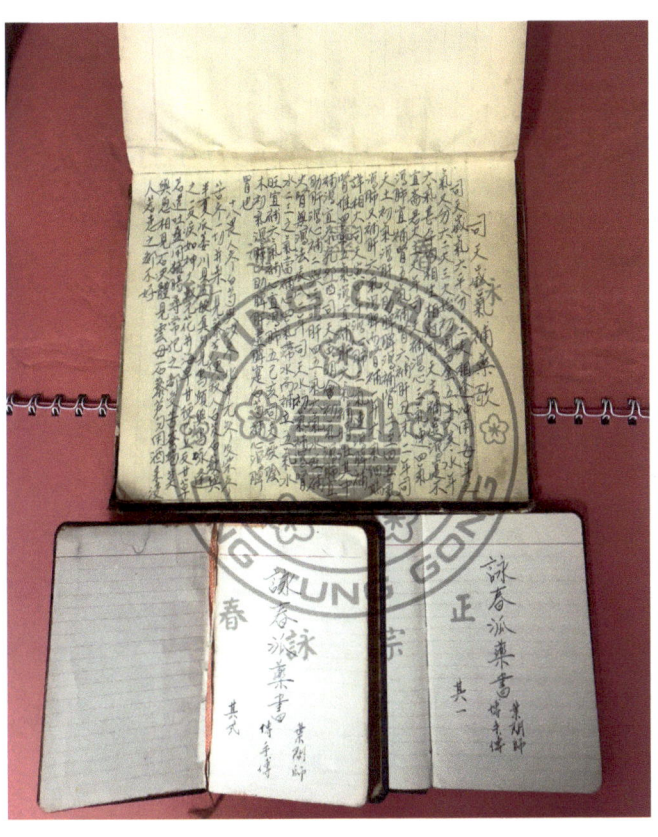

Grand Master Choi emigrated to Australia in the late 1959 and at the time only taught a few friends privately. But after a visit back to Hong Kong early in 1972, GGM Ip Man asked GM Choi to open a wing chun school here in Australia, reluctantly he agreed as he had no interest in teaching formally, but as his Master had requested it he diligently obeyed, but said that he would teach only for five years then pass the school over to his students. Which is exactly what he did, and so the first Australian Wing Chun school opened as the VCK Kung Fu Centre in 768 George Street Sydney. This school closed in the late 1970's.

Over the decades he has continuously studied and refined Wing Chun Ling Tong Gong, and since then has privately taught only a handful of students who sought him out.

Now these teachings are being translated into English by Grandmaster Choi and myself through many hours of lessons and numerous Yum Cha. I am humbled and honoured to have been chosen as Grandmaster Choi's last student and the representative for Wing Chun Ling Tung Gong. I look forward to showing the world another facet of the Wing Chun system & helping other people gain the multitude of health benefits through this wonderful art if they so choose.

Sifu continually stressed to me the importance of daily training and how your health should be the biggest consideration when training Ling Tung Gong.

If somebody only wants to learn the fighting methods of Wing Chun then that's ok also, but they will not have the same ability that comes from training our complete method. The words 靈通 Ling Tung have a vast depth of meaning that I hope to share with you in a future article, but for the time being I will use the simple explanation that they have the meaning of Fast and Abundant, Clever or Effective.

This leads us to the understanding that Wing Chun Ling Tung Gong is a Natural, Fast and Effective method that provides abundant health and wellbeing through the combination of both Wing Chun Qi Gong & Wing Chun Kuen. Couple this with healthy eating and good lifestyle, then amazing happiness and longevity is also achievable.

Because in the end, it's not about what you can get or learn from someone, the question is:

"What can you develop in yourself that can be used to help each other?"

If you are interested in learning more about Wing Chun Ling Tung Gong, send me a message at sifu@kungfusouthside.com.au or find me on Facebook.

Relax, Be Happy, Concentrate, Don't Worry & Persevere.

-Sifu Dave Richardson

Sifu with David Richardson

Introduction to Capoeira
by Nathaniel Mitchell

Capoeira, a martial art that seamlessly blends combat, dance, music, and acrobatics, is a vivid tapestry of Brazilian culture with a rich, complex history. As a seasoned martial arts practitioner with three decades of experience, I have witnessed the evolution of various martial arts, but the story of capoeira stands unique in its history, depth, and resilience.

Tracing its roots back to the 16th century, capoeira emerged amongst African slaves in Brazil. Its predecessor arts were various systems of movement from across the continent: wrestling, dance, fights set in a ring, fights set to music; the historical links are endless. During the slave trade, individuals from various countries were rounded up and found themselves in Bahia, Brazil; a major landing port for slave ships. In this melting pot of cultures, traditions, religions, and languages, people saw a common thread. They pulled them together, and in various clandestine spaces, capoeira was born. It became a source of camaraderie amongst disparate people, a symbol of resistance and hope against the brutal conditions of slavery. Disguised as a dance with musical traditions as rich as the movements themselves, capoeira enabled slaves to practice fighting techniques without arousing the suspicion of their oppressors. This early form of capoeira was raw and survival-focused, far from the more structured discipline we see today.

In contrast, Mestre Pastinha championed "Capoeira Angola," which adhered more closely to the traditions and rituals of the ancestral form.

He opened the Centro Esportivo de Capoeira Angola, preserving the traditional elements like the ritualistic "roda," music, and ceremonial aspects, which are integral to the spirit of capoeira. He was able to licence his school as a dance school, quite differently to that of the Capoeira Regional school.

Although not formalised like the Capoeira Regional training regimen, Angola has a history of teaching lineages associated with it which can be traced back to slaves who practiced it. In this way, a divide opened in capoeira between the 'formal' style of Capoeira Regional and the historical style of Capoeira Angola. That said, the two major styles share songs, rituals, movements, and instruments. To the untrained eye, both styles look similar. More modern styles have amalgamated these two lineages, calling themselves Capoeira Contemporânea (contemporary capoeira), or found themselves stemming from still different roots, like Capoeira Banguela. For this article, however, we're only going to talk about Capoeira as Regional and Angola.

Capoeira's journey from a forbidden practice to a celebrated art form is a testament to its resilience and adaptability. The UNESCO's recognition of the roda, the circular formation within which capoeira is practiced, as an Intangible Cultural Heritage of Humanity in 2014, marked a significant milestone. It highlighted the cultural and historical importance of capoeira, not just as a martial art but as a symbol of identity, resistance, and artistry.

""My message is that they have to embrace capoeira with all their hearts because capoeira has a lot to offer to the people who dedicate themselves. The more you devote to capoeira, the more capoeira will return to you."
Mestre Paulo

In recent years, organizations like Red Bull have included capoeira in their global sporting events. This inclusion has not only provided a platform for capoeira practitioners to showcase their skill but also helped in introducing this art form to a broader, more diverse audience.

For martial artists from other disciplines, capoeira offers a unique perspective. It's not just about physical prowess; it's about rhythm, history, and community. It challenges practitioners to not only engage their bodies but also their minds and spirits in a harmonious dance of resilience and grace. As it continues to evolve and influence, capoeira remains a vibrant reminder of the power of cultural expression and the unyielding spirit of the human will.

Capoeira's journey to Australia began in the late 20th century, with Brazilian immigrants and visiting masters introducing this art form. Over the years, it has evolved from being a novel cultural import to a significant element of Australia's diverse cultural scene. Several schools can be found in all major cities in Australia, including Darwin. Simply search on Facebook for capoeira in your city (note the spelling of capoeira).

Also, there's a hub for Australia capoeira called, you guessed it, Capoeira Australia and Capoeira Hub (both are Facebook groups). The admins are from those various schools around Australia, and they attempt to give a complete and unbiased access to capoeira events and meetings as they happen.

Depending on your kind of experience and your own body, different types of capoeira may be more your style.

Styles of Capoeira
- Capoeira Angola: Known for its fluid, close-to-the-ground movements and traditional roots, emphasizing cunning, strategy, and tradition.
- Capoeira Regional: Developed by Mestre Bimba, showcasing rapid, athletic movements, more martial and acrobatic.
- Banguela: A slower, more playful rhythm than Regional, allowing players more time to strategize and interact.
- Contemporânea: A blend of Angola and Regional, offering a versatile and adaptive form of Capoeira.

Capoeira in Australia is a cultural phenomenon that bridges communities and cultures. Its evolution reflects the dynamic, multicultural fabric of Australian society. As it continues to grow, Capoeira remains a vibrant testament to the power of cultural exchange and the universal appeal of this unique art form.

Capoeira in Australian
- Facebook Groups: Platforms like "Capoeira Australia" serve as online communities for sharing events and fostering connections.
- Capoeira Hub Australia: A central news platform for national Capoeira events and achievements.
- Instagram Feeds: Personal accounts showcasing techniques, performances, and the cultural aspects of Capoeira.
- Spotify Playlists: Collections of Capoeira music, from traditional toques to contemporary compositions, enhancing the practice and appreciation of the art.

Keiko Fukuda (1913-2013): The first woman to attain the 10th dan in judo, Fukuda dedicated her life to promoting women's participation in martial arts. Despite facing significant gender discrimination, she persevered and became a symbol of resilience and dedication for judokas worldwide.

Jigoro Kano (Judo):
The founder of Judo, Kano revolutionized martial arts by developing a system that could be practiced safely as a sport. He emphasized the principle of "maximum efficiency with minimum effort."

Gichin Funakoshi (Karate):
Often called the "Father of Modern Karate," Funakoshi played a crucial role in introducing karate to mainland Japan and emphasizing its character-building aspects.

Yip Man (Wing Chun):
A grandmaster of Wing Chun and teacher of Bruce Lee, Yip Man was known for his skill and his efforts to preserve and spread Wing Chun during turbulent times in China.

Helio Gracie (Brazilian Jiu-Jitsu):
Co-founder of Brazilian Jiu-Jitsu, Gracie adapted traditional Japanese jujutsu to create a highly effective ground-fighting system. Like Musashi, he emphasised technique over strength.

Sun Lutang (Tai Chi):
A master of multiple Chinese martial arts, Sun created Sun-style Tai Chi and wrote influential books on martial arts theory and practice.

Chojun Miyagi (Goju-Ryu Karate):
Founder of Goju-Ryu Karate, Miyagi integrated hard and soft techniques and emphasized the importance of both physical and spiritual development.

Mas Oyama (Kyokushin Karate):
Founder of Kyokushin Karate, Oyama was known for his incredible physical feats and his development of a hard-hitting, full-contact style of karate.

Morihei Ueshiba (Aikido):

Founder of Aikido, Ueshiba developed a martial art that emphasizes harmony and non-violence. Like Musashi, he wrote extensively about his philosophy, blending martial techniques with spiritual principles.

Bruce Lee (Jeet Kune Do):
While more modern, Lee's impact on martial arts philosophy is comparable to Musashi's. He developed Jeet Kune Do as a hybrid martial art and philosophy, emphasising adaptability and efficiency.

West Coast Aikido Inspiration

by Duncan Mitchell

I have been practising Aikido at West Coast Aikido Academy in Wangara Perth for a couple of years now following a stroke in 2016. My mobility and fitness are still nowhere near my previous levels, but I get by.

All the senior belts and instructors have been extremely supportive but I want to highlight the inspiration and life lessons I've had from Sensei Claude the senior instructor under Sensei Ross Taylor, both Ross and Claude are aware of my physical limitations and teach me to adapt techniques to make them work for me. I try to replicate the correct form as best I can, but when this isn't possible, I look for how I can still use the fundamental principles to adapt and still achieve the desired outcome.

This is a lesson which goes beyond the Dojo and reminds me of a book by a famous Golf physiologist Bob Rotella, 'Golf is not a game of Perfect!' we can all learn to 'play it as it lies,' as they say in Golf. In life, things are never going to always be perfect but it's how we face things and adapt to do the best we can, which is important. Aikido has taught me to apply the fundamental principles and work within my physical ability to get results. That doesn't mean I don't try to push myself to always improve, but it has taught me to be flexible and resilient, looking to adapt to each challenge along the way. Never giving up and fighting through adversity are some of the key points Sensei Claude has taught me. His encouragement and direction help me push forward to achieve my martial arts goals. He is a strong believer in putting passion into the practice and performing techniques with purpose rather than just going through the motions, he doesn't go easy on me and we often have a laugh when demonstrating a technique saying how he's looking forward to seeing how I get along with this one, particularly when it involves kneeling.

His belief that I can attempt techniques has given me a boost to try harder inside and outside the dojo.

Shu-Ha-Rei
The True Concept of Advancement in the Japanese Martial Arts
Budo - Bujutsu - Heiho

by Tim Nicklin

Today in martial arts such as Karate, Judo, Aikido ad infinitum et cetera… people mainly only recognize the colour belt system of advancement, however in reality the colour belt (Obi) system is a false system made up for modern sport and is not a traditional advancement system of the older (Koryu) styles of Bujutsu, such as Kobujutsu, Karate jutsu or Jujutsu et alia, in fact the idea of the modern belt system comes from a Chinese/Japanese board game known as Go.

The now famous colour belt system was invented by Kano Jigoro Sensei of Judo fame in 1883. Kano was looking to create a reward system for his modern art/sport of Judo (soft way) and not trying to override the existing system of advancement in the Budo (martial way) of advancement known as the licensed system (menkyo) which we can look at in the future, however for now I wish to explain in brief the more esoteric advancement through the life training idea of Shu, Ha, Ri.

However, looking for Japanese recognition, the Okinawan art of Toudi (karate) adopted the same system and so the colour belt system started to spread to most of the modern arts we recognize today as martial arts.

As mentioned apart from the physical achievement of gaining a license, there was and still is a much more esoteric view of advancement held to heart by a few lifelong traditionalists of martial artist who have passed through the modern sport idea and transcended art to martial arts real meanings of a life spent in development.

The three stages of training

守破離

Shu: the first stage is the stage of learning that can mean either obey or protect, and in this stage of the learning process, it is essential that the student obeys his/her Sensei in all their training mannerism. This allows the Sensei to fully protect the student from any corruption in their training (the teaching process or passing on of knowledge will always involve some corruption and we must take care to spot and stop this corruption). The Shu stage of training will or should concern itself totally with the rudimentary (shoho) of the art in question and it is important that the relationship of teacher and student be more of parent and child rather than colleagues in a university atmosphere where on occasions, the line may be crossed in terms of conversational learning through open lecture on the mannerisms of the subject at hand.

Here in Shu, the question of why or what's the meaning of this is not applicable and in reality, would assimilate to a child asking a grandparent Hamlet's question of, "to be or not to be that is the question" i.e. what's the meaning of life. The student should concentrate purely on getting all the postures (shisei) and transitions through postures (dosa) as correct as possible, whilst the Sensei should try not to muddy the waters so to speak with complicated unnecessary applications they mistakenly call Bunkai (Bunkai means analysis or reduction not application).

Keeping to these rather strict boundaries which most are unfamiliar with today will serve in great magnitudes when it comes to pure skill building and will actually add a depth of knowledge otherwise unattainable to the student as the foundation supplied by this (shoho) rudimentary foundation building is going to serve as priceless in the two stages to come especially in the final stage.

Ha: this is another stage where the term used has a dualistic meaning. This term can either mean break as in breaking free or frustrate as in the student frustrating the Sensei by bombarding them with questions on every level. At this stage, the student will try to break free of the strict regime of shoho (rudimentary) used in the first stage of Shu. This is where Hamlet's question of the meaning of life (life in karate) will and does get continually asked as the student (gakusei) tries the break free and starts to apply their own understanding to techniques learnt in the beginning stage. To keep the student on the right track the Sensei will have to start teaching the principles (shugi) of the technique (waza), this will naturally change the relationship into a more two-way relationship and the Sensei must start to treat the student as an adult, whilst still commanding the respect of a teacher. This change in relationship is frustrating for many modern teachers who just instruct and can't actually teach in any depth.

The true Sensei starts to really see the character of the individual students at this point of the training process, however many students will drop out at this point some through frustration themselves at the lengthy process of traditional training (dento-teki renshu) and some with the immature misunderstanding of thinking that the change in relationship means they have made it to the senior stages of training (this in my opinion can and has caused a problem for the future development of martial arts). This stage has no time limit set to it as nor does the first and advancement depends purely on the student's capability of coming to terms with and understanding what it means to be living within a tradition system of martial arts and not just playing a sport, as they should start to understand the colour of the belt does not define or trap the individual student and the Sensei will teach appropriately according to each student's capabilities. It is easy to see why this stage is called breaking and frustrating.

Ri: is the final stage of learning and surprisingly has a dualistic meaning in terms of martial arts. It can mean either separate or set free from. At this stage the Sensei and student tend to separate from each in terms of daily or weekly training as the student, now a senior black belt of long standing (Kodansha) and having spent many years in the previous two stages has absorbed all they are going to through daily or weekly training with their master. The Master will also feel that he/she has little to give by carrying on with daily or weekly training and that it is time for the student in question to start on the deeper inward journey of self-development through personal study and training and teaching to others in their own right (which as some will already know is a massive learning curve in its own way). At this final and everlasting stage, it would be true to think that the relationship between teacher master and teacher student is over because it's not, even though now both operating in different fields of endeavor the connection between the two should become stronger than ever. They will still follow their own paths as individuals but the two will still be joined in mutual respect and conversation and learning will continue until old age or deaths separates them from each other, the kanji (Chinese character used in Japanese writing) that represents this last stage is written with the same kanji as magaki (a rough woven fence or bamboo hedge). So, one can see that no matter how far student and teacher are separated, there will always be this fence to walk to where they can find each other whether physically or spiritually.

In this more traditional esoteric style of advancement, one should not be worried too much about the colour of one's belt, as the colours change from style-to-style club to club.

Rather I am writing here of a bygone age where Sensei was a highly respected person in the community and their students were handpicked or recommended to the Sensei in question by other leading members of the community. It should also be said that this system of advancement far predates the modern system of commercial belts aimed at sport recognition.

SHU: Obey Protect

HA: Break-Frustrate

RI: Separate Set Free

Me and my teaching staff on the week I left England 2007

Me & my best man with my Shotokan - KobuJutsu Sensei Roger Stephens

Author Tim Nicklin 7th Dan
NIWA Dojo Western Australia

How I Came to Learn Krav Maga
& began teaching others

by Richard Brandt

In 2018 I decided to finally make good on a long-held ambition to take up a martial art. I had always admired those who did martial arts, with many school friends doing stints in Karate, ever popular in the 90s. How someone could execute the speed and precision to defend and strike always fascinated me, but I never seriously nagged my parents to take me to any classes. Much later, as an adult, I found myself living alone, having not owned a TV for years, no kids, no pets, no more excuses. I had to fill my evenings with something and scratching along trying to learn to play guitar on my own wasn't cutting it. It seemed unlikely I would ever have more time or opportunity to commit to it and felt I had better get onto it while I was still somewhat young. I was 34.

Originally, my intention was to train Muay Thai, because I was a massive Tony Jaa fan. But also because Muay Thai has a reputation for its ferocity. It's possible it being one of the most available and marketed arts in the West contributed to this decision, but that would have been subconscious. I confessed my ambition to a friend while we were out for dinner one weekend having a periodic catch up. He vetoed my stance on Muay Thai, countering with "if I was going to do any of them, I'd do Krav Maga." I had never heard of it and when he told me it was from Israel, I said "well, those guys don't mess around, that's the one for me."

For those not familiar, Krav Maga is a hand-to-hand combat system conceived by Imi Lichtenfeld post World War II and has since been adopted by the Israel Defence Force. It borrows the most effective techniques from various combat arts and rolls them into one hyper-effective system for the preservation of life in violent situations. Based on boxing, Greco-Roman wrestling and Aikido, at its most extreme Krav Maga features aggressive high and low striking and emphasises forward and continuous movement to take out an attacker as efficiently as possible. Defending and using objects as weapons, takedowns and restraints can all form the curriculum making it just about the most comprehensive system I have seen.

As luck would have it, there was a large Krav Maga gym in the area and we even walked past it after that very dinner. I remember walking past the large glass door to the old warehouse building in a side street in inner Sydney, sign written with the gym's logo in military colours. It looked so dark and ominous. It said this was the real deal. When later that week I researched the place looking to sign up, it turned out there was another branch of the same gym just up the road from my place. It was destiny. I went to a trial class and never looked back.

For me the appeal in martial arts was always about self defence. When I was thinking to do Muay Thai, unbeknownst to me at the time what I was really wanted to do was Muay

Boran, the ancient form of unarmed combat practised by warriors and villagers in ancient Thailand. This art is now largely untaught in favour of the modern version of Thai boxing most are familiar with (though there is now a push by the Thai government to preserve this cultural treasure before it is lost). I immediately loved Krav's no non-sense approach to training real scenarios as well as its more casual attitude by doing away with martial arts customs and traditions such as specific clothing, asking permission and bowing to walk onto the mat and so on. We wore regular clothes, as that was what we would be executing the techniques in should a situation ever call for it. We bowed in and out of class together, and that was it. And while there was a uniform of sorts, it was just a plain black tee with the gym name printed on the front. Simple. The gym taught striking with hands and legs, weapons defences, stand-up grappling and ground grappling with an emphasis on escape over submissions. Far more than you tend to get elsewhere.

After that initial trial class, I started with an eight-class pass and burned through that pretty quickly. I then noticed a lot of the newer people who started around the same time as me began training almost every night. The way the class pass was priced meant that if you did two classes per week, you had paid just over a regular membership which granted you unlimited classes. And with classes on every day, this seemed a no-brainer. What started as a commitment for an hour twice per week became a nightly routine and often Saturdays as well. Before long, my peers and I joined the advanced program and were training 2+ hours a day. Naturally, skill acquisition correlated with mat time (not always the case with some!). Within 20 months, I had done a training camp in Tel Aviv, began instructor training and ultimately certified as an instructor myself. Just under one year on, I certified as a senior instructor. I've helped hundreds of people reach trying levels of competency in Krav, most of whom, like me, had no other experience in martial arts. Some even went on to become instructors themselves.

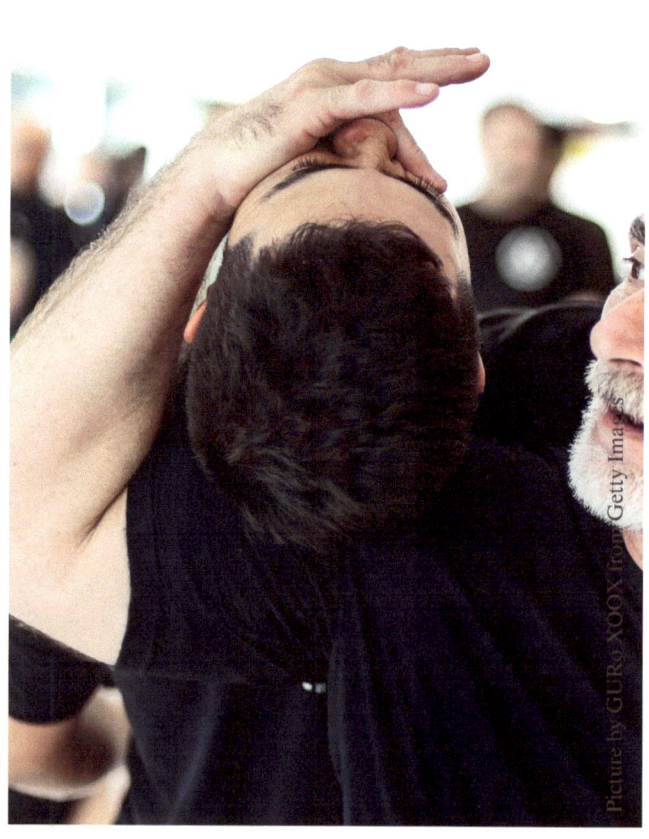

The funny thing about Krav is that because it teaches all these what I call "macro skills", the usual outcome is people have a broad knowledge and become capable in many skills, but never really master any of them. Krav won't make you a pro boxer or grappler, for example. But my Krav training did mean I have been able to walk into many big name location gyms overseas and hold my own. I always had great feedback on my skills and speed knowledge, which is a testament to how well I was taught more than anything. My trainers took me from a guy off the street with zero experience to someone apparently capable of handling themselves to some degree in a short time, exactly what Krav was created to do.

Which leads to a major point. If taught well, Krav is a great all-round system to learn. It will teach you skills that will hold up in a sports-focussed gym, such as Jiu Jitsu or kickboxing. But make no mistake, while you might be too practised for the beginner's class in such places, you will likely be destroyed by the experienced people there! Unfortunately, however, good Krav Maga seems to be hard to come by and I have seen a lot of low quality and, frankly, incorrect teaching going on lately. The reasons for this are many and probably for another article, but this issue ultimately led me to stepping down from my regular teaching post at the very gym I started with to take a break from training Krav Maga. Without many options to train Krav Maga worldwide, a pathway back is going to take some time.

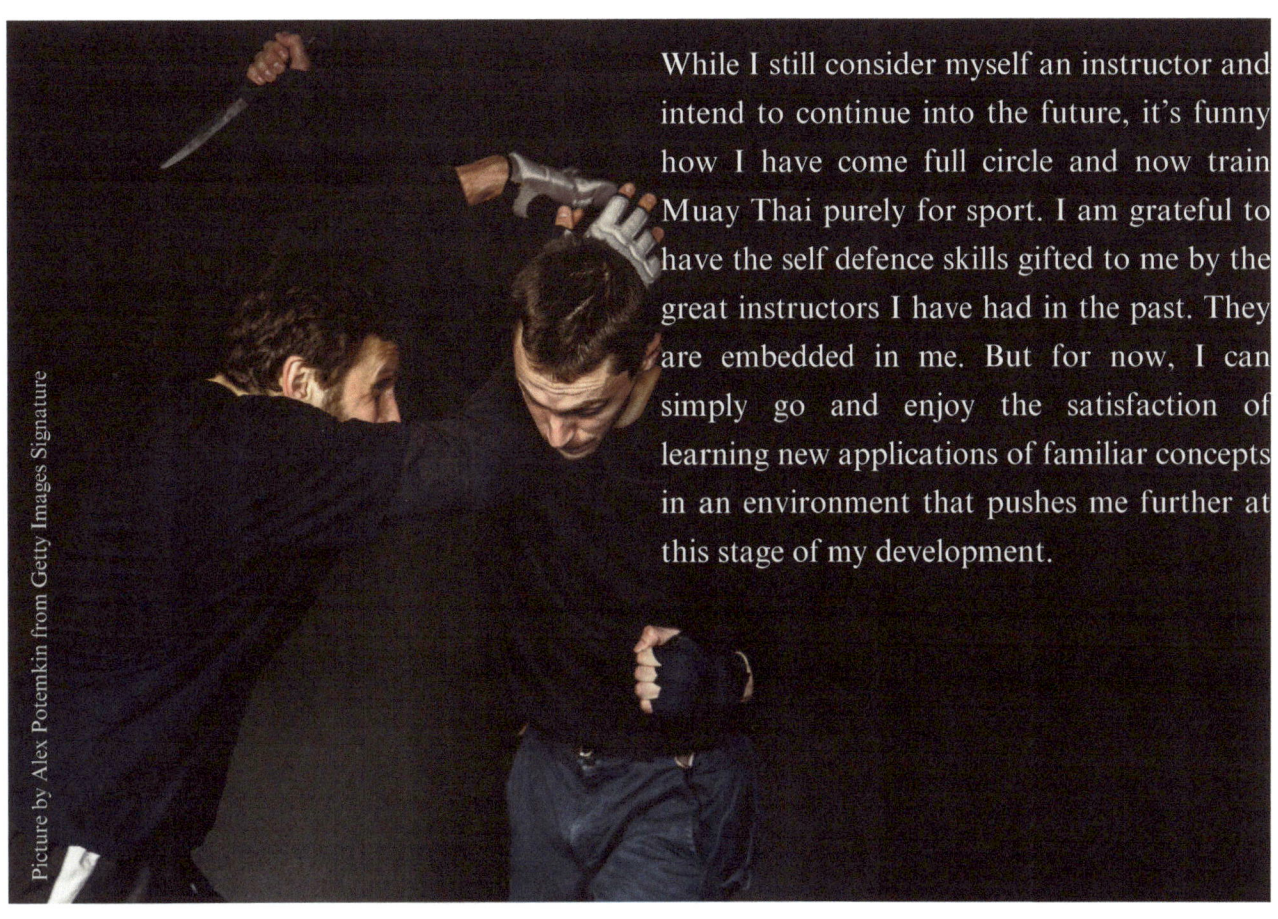

Picture by Alex Potemkin from Getty Images Signature

While I still consider myself an instructor and intend to continue into the future, it's funny how I have come full circle and now train Muay Thai purely for sport. I am grateful to have the self defence skills gifted to me by the great instructors I have had in the past. They are embedded in me. But for now, I can simply go and enjoy the satisfaction of learning new applications of familiar concepts in an environment that pushes me further at this stage of my development.

Kaiya entered into the world of Brazilian Jiu-Jitsu (BJJ) started around June 2021. Instantly falling in love with the sport and competition side of it. She has proven herself to be an exceptionally talented young girl. Kaiya is 9-year-old and trains and competes out of PMC (Perth Martial Arts Centre) based in Perth Western Australia under the expert guidance of Master Goioere Dias and Professor William Dias. Kaiya has garnered an impressive record thus far of 29 consecutive gold medals since commencing as a 6-year-old and holds an outstanding record of 51 matches with 45 wins by way of submissions. She competes regularly in Gi and No-Gi events and has been victorious against girls that are older, heavier, higher rank and boys her age. She has not lost a single match since October 2021 which is impressive!

Kaiya is the current Pan Pacific international title holder and a 6x Western Australia state title holder. Her ongoing hard work, success and determination have led her to qualify for the AJP Youth Gi World Championships in Abu Dhabi UAE scheduled for November 2024, where she is determined to make her mark as a junior world champion. She has set her sights on competing at the highest level and achieving her dream of becoming a Brazilian Jiu-Jitsu black belt and World Champion. We are also planning to travel and take her to competitions in Sydney in July, Australian Nationals in Melbourne in August and Bali in September 2024 to give her more experience. Her 10-year old sister Kora also trains and competes and is a WA state champion. Guess it's in the blood with mum and dad both being ex-professional muay thai champions.

We are also seeking sponsors to help get Kaiya to the world BJJ competition in November in Abu Dhabi we can be contacted via info@martialartsmagazineaustralia.com

Meet Tiana, Kaiya's Mum
Talent does run in the family

I began 'kickboxing' as it was called back in the day in Perth in 1994 in high school, around 17 years of age. I fell in love with martial arts immediately and have been doing it ever since! I achieved my black singlet, and then switched styles to Kenpo Karate. It took me about five years to gain my black belt in that.

I travelled to Sydney for work and trained and started competing whilst there. I returned to Perth and started Muay Thai under my instructor Bill Seth (Kru) at Mungkorn Mai Muay Thai. I started competing in Muay Thai around the age of 25 and quickly became addicted. I then spent the next ten years travelling, competing in that sport and lived in Thailand for a period of time too. I was fortunate enough to work in a Muay Thai gym in Singapore for a a while. During my time I had a total of 47 fights in kickboxing, muay Thai and boxing and I won numerous WA state, Australian, Intercontinental, South Pacific titles under WMC and WBC. The highlight was winning the prestigious Kings Cup in Thailand in 2008.

When I returned to Perth, I trained up for my first WBC (World Boxing Council) Muay Thai bantamweight world title. I won that in 2011 against a girl from Japan, and defended it in 2012 against a girl from Thailand, before travelling to Los Vegas in America for my final fight. I then retired from the sport and had children.

Two and a half years ago my two daughters, aged nine and ten started their own martial arts journey in Brazilian Jiu-Jitsu (BJJ) in Perth under Perth Martial Arts Centre based in Malaga/Ellenbook. It is lovely to see my children now fall in love with martial arts that has been my passion since I was young. It is good for them in so many ways, developing discipline, resilience, persistence, loyalty, self-defence, confidence, friendships and creating a healthy lifestyle. I now also train alongside them myself and recently achieved my white belt (2 stripes)! And it is definitely a lot different and harder than expected but I enjoy now learning 'the ground game'.

My girls are both WA state champions and the youngest who has a great passion for BJJ is now 6 x WA state champion, 1 x International Pan Pacs champion and looking at going to the nationals in Melbourne and worlds in Abu Dhabi later in the year. I find the competing aspect of it gives their training focus, goals and to be the best version of themselves.

Martial Arts versus Self Defence
by Leanne Canning

What is martial arts vs self defence? As a Martial artist you have probably come across the debate that martial arts and self-defence the same thing. Let's take a sneak peak at the difference before we get started.

When I think about martial arts I think of it as consensual violence. Martial arts has a belt rank system and combines a mixture of modern and traditional arts. The combined practices of combat were practiced for a variety of reasons such as self-defence, competition, military training, physical, mentally and spiritually. Each style of martial arts has its own technical skills of strikes, kicks, blocks, defences or take-downs.

Over the years, many martial arts styles e.g. karate, Taekwondo, Judo and Brazilian jiujitsu have been adapted for competition. Intense sparring sessions and kata from karate & Taekwondo or the impressive grappling skills of judo or BJJ. Although these styles can be effective for self-defence situations. A martial artist needs to have both the physical and mental strength to be able to adapt each technique to make it work in any given situation.

On the other hand self-defence is known as non-consensual violence. It is the use of physical force to counterattack or de-escalate an immediate threat of violence. But by law cannot be done by using excessive force, causing serious bodily harm or death.

Despite what many combat sport and traditional sensei's say, there is a distinct different between practicing martial arts and self-defence. While often taught as one and the same, they have fundamentally distinct skills with different objectives and methodologies. This article aims to shed light on these differences, highlighting some of the unique aspects of each practice.

Martial arts is classed as a form of consensual violence where practitioners agree to engage in sparring matches under a set of predefined rules. This controlled environment is designed to ensure the safety of the practitioners while allowing them to practice and demonstrate their technical abilities. These rules include restrictions on what types of strikes can be used, targets to the body, weight class, amount of force and usually includes a time limit. There is also the presence of referees who ensure rules are not broken and a sparring match is halted if the practitioner is at risk of any serious injury.

In stark contrast, self-defence is about responding to non-consensual violence. Remember there are no rules involved and attackers would use the element of surprise, to make sure you are your most vulnerable. In this situation the primary goal is not to demonstrate skills or win a medal but to protect oneself from any potential injury and escape to safety.

In order to add these skills into your martial arts training. You need to set up real life simulation of an attack (with safety measures) and see how you would react. This could be done not only with adults but also kids. But using different scenarios for each age group. It is important to get in touch with your fight or flight response. Giving you a chance to adjust your techniques by learning your strengths or weaknesses and improving each time.

Martial arts sparring could be classed as wilful engagement. This because when you spar inside the dojo or for competitive reasons. You are aware of the following:

1. You both agreed to the fight and it's becomes more about winning, rather than causing injury to your opponent. This is clearly shown in competitive arts like Taekwondo, Brazilian jiujitsu, Judo and Karate.
2. You're only focused on winning by using legal techniques allowed in your martial arts system. Therefore, because the fight is stopped after a point has been rewarded you are actually increases the amount of time you fight. By doing this it greatly increases your chances of losing, which you cannot afford to do in any self-defence situation especially when a weapon is involved.

On the other hand is more of a defensive strategy with the goal of deflecting the immediate danger and escaping before another strike can occur. While martial arts uses fancy techniques, like spin kicks etc. In a self-defence scenario you would be wise to only stick with the basics.

Otherwise if you used most martial arts techniques with excessive force and caused grievous bodily harm or death. You would be penalised by the law. Self-defence is an act of survival – not a 'fist fight'.

Self-defence also differs to a sport / martial arts sparring match by missing several factors:

1. Awareness – Both parties are fully aware of the fight ahead of time.
2. Preparation – Mental, emotional, and physical preparation is done far in advance.
3. Consent – There will be prior arrangements that both people will fight at a specific time and place.
4. Rules / Environment – Safety rules (no illegal moves, no multiple attackers, etc), time limits / rounds, presence of referee, takes place in a safe environment free of any dangerous objects or bad terrain. All these factors stop someone from being seriously injured or killed.

The mindset is also different when approaching martial arts vs self-defence. Think about this in martial arts you know you what skills and techniques will be used and you know you won't get hurt. You know your attacker and you have protective gear like gloves, mouth guard, helmet and mats. Also when you spar it is only a one on one situation where in real life you could have multiple attackers.

You never want a martial arts student having a false sense of security. Often if not taught they will attempt to fight instead of run, believing they can handle themselves. In addition, training could actually interfere with your threat assessment because you are already trained in a particular style.

Especially with younger children, as they are training against people of the same age. Not a grown adult with way more power and weight ratio. When I started doing martial arts, I actually preferred training with guys, because I knew they were who I would need to escape from in a real life scenario. All the guys were so helpful in guidance of how I could adjust and improve my techniques to get better. One of my best sparring partners used to call me his arch nemesis. Because we were always trying to out do each other.

We can look at the self-defence mindset in two different ways. We cannot control how, where, or why we are attacked. A perpetrator will try to catch you off guard and when you are most vulnerable. They may have a weapon and multiple attackers can occur. Environmental factors can come to play such surface tension and confined areas. All these things will affect how you fight, your mindset and chances of survival.

Also if we look at it from a domestic violence perspective. Yes, you will know your attacker but now you also have an emotional connection to the person wishing to cause you harm. Maybe your kids are even in the same room and let's not forget the emotional, mental and physical torment you have been exposed to is not a once off. But has been building and escalating for months or even years.

Martial arts will teach you not only weapon defence against a gun, knife or stick. But also how to fight with weapons like karate with bo sticks, sai and nunchucks. But let's remember these weapons are illegal to use outside of the dojo.

Here is Australia it's basically illegal to carry anything for self-defence. Even self-defence keychains can be a grey area. While they aren't explicitly banned, any device designed to cause harm could potentially be considered a weapon under Australian law. So we need to rely on our martial arts or self-defence skills in order to defend ourselves.

In a self-defence situation, most of your martial arts training will go out the window if there's a weapon involved. When I have done knife defence training basics, they teach you how to deflect the knife and disarm. But the problem is that we always trained in a way where you can always see the knife.

After doing a lot of research I discovered that the majority of knife attacks occur when a knife is pulled in the middle of an attack. And are likely to be stabbed at least three times before you're even aware it has occurred.

That is why it's better that if you are held at knife point for a robbery or car jacking to give the attacker exactly what they want. Phone, wallet, purse, doesn't matter. These items can always be replaced, unlike your life.

Most martial artist systems out there take roughly 5-6 years to earn their Black belts. Whereas Brazilian jiujitsu practitioners can take ten years or more. I was always taught when I started karate that black belt is like getting your white belt all over again. As this when the real training begins.

Self-defence classes can generally range from a couple of weeks up to a month depending where the classes are held. It is important to remember that just like a martial artist, if you stop training over a period of time your skill set will decline overtime. Which can leave you vulnerable if you find yourself in a dangerous situation. I would highly recommend to retake self-defence classes once a year, just to keep your techniques fresh. Also note both martial arts and self-defence requires not just physical ability but a high mental strength.

By understanding that martial arts vs self-defence is a crucial aspect for anyone interested in personal protection and combat training. Martial arts offer a structured approach to learning combat techniques within a rule-based system, focusing on physical skills and mental discipline.

Self-defence, is about survival in unpredictable, non-consensual confrontations. It requires a broader mindset and skill level that includes awareness, de-escalation techniques, legal knowledge, and strategies for dealing with multiple attackers

A lot of martial arts overtime has become a lot more focused on competing at high levels. Therefore, some of lost the traditional practices of self defence.

Self-defence training is far more geared to protecting yourself and loved ones in a 'street' context. In addition, no martial art style or self-defence system will ever be able to teach you everything you need to know about the complexities of violence especially when involved in a high risk situation.

The goal is to teach people how to avoid conflict by using mental and physical skills. That allow them to de-escalate potentially dangerous situations when necessary.
And of course, if required to physically defend yourself or your loved ones. I have always said that your instructor can teach a lot of vital skills and a share of knowledge. But it is up-to you as a students to put those skills to practice. By always working out how to improve by adjusting and testing your skills over an over again.

MATAYOSHI KOBUDO

Part I & II

by Bryan H. Wiratno

PART I

Kobudo is the forgotten brother of karate. When karate changed from "Tang/chinese hand (唐手)" to "empty hand (空手)," the art of weaponry originally practised by the old masters of karate started to slowly vanish. Kanga "Tode" Sakugawa was famous for his bojutsu, his student Sokon Matsumura, and later Matsumura's student Anko Azato, were noted masters of Jigen-ryu, a sword-fighting art brought to Okinawa by the Satsuma samurais. The Motobu brothers, Choyu and Choki, both also practised Jigen-ryu [10] while Chotoku Kyan practised bojutsu and taught it to all of his students. Even Gichin Funakoshi brought bojutsu with him when he first came to mainland Japan, something modern karateka seem to have conveniently forgotten. Perhaps the oldest reference we have of kobudo being practised together with karate is Chatan Yara, from the 17th century, who practised bo, sai, and eku (oar). Chatan Yara no Sai is still a kata performed in several styles to this day.

Kobudo means "ancient martial art," which, let's be honest, is a very generic name that sheds no light whatsoever. In this context, what it refers to is actually the weaponry of Okinawa, the rokushaku bo (6-feet staff) being the most ubiquitous. The history of kobudo is actually very intricate and murky, similar to the history of prewar karate.

There are, however, some things about kobudo's history that we do know of. A prevailing myth is that kobudo was only practised by farmers using their farming tools after the Satsuma banned weapons in Okinawa. We know this to be false as most kobudo masters were nearly all part of the Yukatchu (aristocratic) and Aji (royalty) classes, Sanra Chinen perhaps being the sole exception [1], just like the karate masters. We can also see this in the prevalent use of metal weapons like the sai, tekko, and tinbe-rochin which would be too expensive for the Heimin (commoner) class.

The three main styles of kobudo are Matayoshi Kobudo, Yamane-ryu, and Ryukyu Kobudo. There are, of course, offshoots of these three styles as well as unique kobudo integrated into karate styles like in Isshin-ryu and Ryuei-ryu. Each of these styles have their own unique characteristics and history.

Ryukyu Kobudo is to kobudo what Shito-ryu is to karate. Taira Shinken created the style to preserve as much traditional okinawan kobudo as he could accumulate, which means that this style has the highest number of kata [11]. The movements of Ryukyu Kobudo also look more standardised and refined, a bit more mainland-influenced. For this reason, it is perhaps the best portrayal of generic kobudo across the Ryukyu Islands.

Taira Shinken originally learned kobudo from Yabiku Moden [12]. Moden was a student of Anko Itosu, but he seemed to have specialised in kobudo. Ryukyu Kobudo was first started to preserve Moden's kobudo, which was mostly based on old-style Yamane-ryu bojutsu, but along the way, Taira seemed to have collected far more kobudo than anyone.

Yamane-ryu (oki: Yamanni-ryu) traditionally only practised the bo, but has recently also incorporated other weapons into the style as well. Yamane-ryu was the kobudo of Chinen Sanra, also called Yamane Tanmei (Grandfather Yamane), Yamane Usume (Old Man Yamane), or Yamane Chinen (Chinen of Yamane), who was a peasant from, as you might have guessed, Yamane [1]. It is not clear where or whom Chinen learned his bojutsu, although one theory is that it came from Kanga Sakugawa. Another theory is that Chinen learned bojutsu from his village and innovated the rest himself. One way or another, Chinen achieved fame for his bojutsu that even the aristocrats learned from him. The style was succeeded by his grandson Masami Chinen.

The defining feature of the style is characterised by the extended grip along with very loose whipping cuts and bouncing off the bo. Unlike most other styles, Yamane-ryu has a focus on fluidity and relaxation. While anyone doing martial arts will be aware that muscling your technique is always bad, Yamane-ryu works in a way that muscling will actually render the technique useless, even to the point of injuring yourself.

Matayoshi Kobudo was kobudo as passed down through the Matayoshi family and finally culminating with Matayoshi Shinko and his son Matayoshi Shinpo. This style has perhaps the most weapons amongst all kobudo styles—albeit not the most kata, that honour belongs to Ryukyu Kobudo—, a lot being farming tools that were not actually made to be weapons such as the kuwa (hoe) and kama (sickle). The style's defining characteristics are the black dogi top and what I like to call "T-rex hands" when gripping the bo. The T-rex hands gives us more flexibility and reach with our strikes, although it is admittedly quite unintuitive at the start and will require a certain degree of wrist mobility that needs some time to get used to. If anyone asks why we wear black dogi, the answer is because weapons that are regularly cleaned and oiled make white dogi dirty really fast. We will discuss more on Matayoshi Kobudo's history and curriculum in part two of this series.

A pattern, not rule, that I have observed personally is that Ryukyu Kobudo tends to be practised by mainland style practitioners, ie Shito-ryu and Shotokan, perhaps due to the close relationship between Taira with Funakoshi and Mabuni. Yamane-ryu tends to be practised by Shorin practitioners, be that of Chibana, Nagamine, or Kyan's lineages. Matayoshi Kobudo tends to be practised by Shorei/Naha-te practitioners. For example

Matayoshi Shinpo himself, Gakiya Yoshiaki, and Hidetada Ishiki all learned Goju-ryu while Takehiro Gaja, Josei Yogi, Shusei Maeshiro, and Takeshi Kinjo are all 9th-10th dan in Uechi-ryu. The background of these masters do seem to have affected the way they each perform their kobudo.

If I were to compare the movements of each kobudo style with boxers, to give a hopefully more relatable picture, whereas Ryukyu Kobudo is the refined Vasyl Lomachenko and Yamane-ryu is the whipping Larry Holmes, Matayoshi Kobudo would be explosive Joe Louis.

PART II

The history of Matayoshi Kobudo as we know it began with Matayoshi Shinko. He learned Kobudo from a young age from his father, Matayoshi Shinchin, and two other teachers, Agena Chokubo and Irei Okina [2]. Later in his twenties, he went to China and learned a style that is now passed down as Kingai-ryu [2]. He would later also learn bojutsu from Yamane Chinen [2] and Ryoko Soeshi [9]. All of that weaponry knowledge would later be synthesised by his son, Matayoshi Shinpo, into the Kobudo style we practise today.

The four main weapons of Matayoshi Kobudo, as well as most other Kobudo styles (with the exception of Yamane-ryu), are the Bo, Sai, Tonfa, and Nunchaku, although the Eku (oar) is regarded as the signature weapon of the Matayoshi family itself [2].

The Matayoshi Eku kata (Tsuken Akachu no Eku di) is probably the only kata originally from the Matayoshi family passed down for more than two generations. Matayoshi Shinpo and Matayoshi Shinko's favourite weapons were the Eku and Kama respectively.

The Nunchaku, perhaps made famous by Bruce Lee, was originally an Okinawan weapon. A common theory is that it was a rice flail turned weapon, another theory is that it is a portable Bo. Matayoshi Kobudo has only one kata, Matayoshi no Nunchaku, and it is characterised by the use of the weapon as both a short-ranged and long-ranged weapon. The Matayoshi Nunchaku has a lot of grip changes that take a great deal of dexterity and confidence to master.

The Tonfa, sometimes also called tunkua, is probably more commonly known as a nightstick, those batons with a grip sticking out from its side that security guards often have. The tonfa was originally from Thailand, although the original mai sok has ropes to tie around the forearm and was used more like a shield or gauntlet than being swung around like in Okinawa or China. We have two tonfa kata created by Matayoshi Shinpo: Tonfa dai Ichi and Tonfa dai Ni. Some branches of Matayoshi Kobudo practise a third kata that was a work in progress, but uncompleted due to Matayoshi Shinpo's death.

The Okinawan Sai came via China from Indonesia, where it is called tekpi or trisula, itself a shortened version of the Indian trident. While the Sai is mainly a stabbing weapon, it is traditionally unsharpened and the prongs are actually used to catch and disarm an enemy's weapon. The Sai, or a mainland variation called the Jutte, was formerly used by the Japanese police. Matayoshi has three sai kata: Ni cho Sai, San cho Sai, and Shinbaru no Sai. The first two were created by Matayoshi Shinpo while Shinbaru no Sai is a traditional kata from Matayoshi Shinko.

This brings us to the most important weapon, not only in Matayoshi, but also all of Kobudo. Like most Okinawan Kobudo styles, we grip the Bo in roughly thirds, unlike the extended grip of Yamane-ryu or Shaolin styles. This is because Matayoshi emphasises the flexibility of using both ends of a weapon at any moment, which is a feature that is also pervasive in all of the style's other weapons as well.

Outside of Matayoshi Kobudo, Matayoshi Shinko and Shinpo taught Kingai-ryu. Kingai-ryu is a chinese kenpo, AKA kung fu, style that Matayoshi Shinko learned in China. Matayoshi Shinpo never really taught Kingai-ryu as a full system and the style is now effectively extinct. One aspect of Kingai-ryu that has been fully preserved in Matayoshi Kobudo is the kama.

That being said, Matayoshi still taught sets of the style to his senior students, leaving them to piece the puzzle together. The leading expert in Kingai-ryu currently is Yoshifumi Hasayaka [9].

The UWA Kobudo Club practises Matayoshi Kobudo as taught by Gakiya Yoshiaki Sensei, Matayoshi Shinpo's chosen successor, and we are affiliated with Yogi Josei Sensei, another of Matayoshi Shinpo's direct students. Sensei Tony Carroll, our head instructor, also studied with Chinen Kenyu Sensei and Gaja Takehiro Sensei for brief periods of time. From these four instructors, Chinen Sensei has a different quality of movement than the rest because of his lineage. Yogi Sensei and Gaja Sensei were both Uechi-ryu practitioners. Chinen Sensei originally learned Shorin-ryu, and kobudo, from Shugoro Nakazato before learning from Matayoshi. Gakiya Sensei has this pouncing-like acceleration curve (muchimi) while Chinen Sensei is more blocky and structured..

As far as syllabus goes, we have five bo kata (Shushi no Kon, Choun no Kon, Sakugawa no Kon, Chikin no Kon, Shishi no Kon), three sai kata, two tonfa kata, and one nunchaku kata (Matayoshi no Nunchaku). On top of kata, we have basic techniques called hojo undo, similar to kihon in other styles, as well as a huge focus on kumi-waza (partner drills, lit: crossing technique). We have three sets of five hojo undo for bo, ten sai hojo undo consisting of six kihon and four combos, ten tonfa hojo undo also consisting of six kihon and four combos, and ten nunchaku hojo undo.

Matayoshi Kobudo, as well as Yamane-ryu, are not quite so rigid in their teachings as most karate styles. If you were to look at videos of different masters performing kata, each of them will have their own tweaks in the kata. Matayoshi Shinpo was infamous for always performing kata differently each time, and Gakiya Sensei also taught differently at different times.

But somehow, despite this rather laissez-faire attitude, the architecture and flavour of the kata are still performed exactly the same. This, to me, is the beauty of Matayoshi Kobudo. It is almost like jazz. We have standards with identifiable melodies, but we are free, and even almost encouraged, to improvise within that context.

With the ever-growing popularity of standardised "sport" karate or, even worse, "performance" karate, I think it is important to remember that Matayoshi Kobudo was, is, and always should be a martial art meant for fighting. Only then can the style be preserved in its entirety, hopefully in the way the Matayoshi family, especially Matayoshi Shinko and Shinpo, would have wanted it to be.

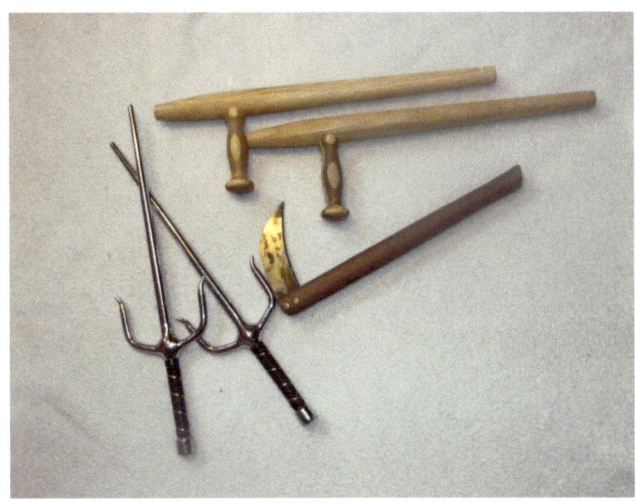

[1] Yamanni-ryu – Is the founder's name Sanrā, Sanda, Masanrā, or Saburō? | RyukyuBugei 琉球武芸
[2] https://kodokanboston.files.wordpress.com/2014/02/meibukanmagazine-no-9_matayoshi.pdf
[3] Shūshi no Kun (Bojutsu Kata Series) — History | Ryukyu Bugei 琉球武芸
[4] The lineage of Shushi nu kun | Thekaratepage.com
[5] The History and Contents of Matayoshi Kobudo as of 1999 | Ryukyu Bugei 琉球武芸
[6] Chōun no Kon (Morning Cloud's Staff) | by Motobu Naoki | Jan, 2024 | Medium
[7] Choun no Kon – (Bojutsu Kata Series) | Ryukyu Bugei 琉球武芸
[8] Chōshi no Kon. Bō kata of Soeishi-ryū | by Motobu Naoki | Motobu-ryu Blog | Dec, 2023 | Medium
[9] Kingai-ryū Karate Okinawa Kobujutsu (Info translated from the Nihon Kobudō Kyōkai, 2022) | Ryukyu Bugei 琉球武芸
[10] Motobu Chōki's Wooden Sword. Written by Motobu Naoki, translated by… | by Motobu Naoki | Motobu-ryu Blog | Medium
[11] Kobudo kata list – then and now | Ryukyu Bugei 琉球武芸
[12] Taira Shinken – Restorer of Okinawa Kobudō | Ryukyu Bugei 琉球武芸
[13] The techniques of Chinen Masami's Yamani-ryū | Ryukyu Bugei 琉球武芸

THE WISDOM OF Mr. Miyagi

by Maria Francis

In the pantheon of martial arts cinema, few characters have left as indelible a mark as Mr. Keisuke Miyagi from The Karate Kid franchise. Portrayed with nuance and depth by the late Pat Morita, Mr. Miyagi transcends the typical martial arts master archetype to become a beacon of wisdom, resilience, and compassion. His impact extends far beyond the realm of karate, offering profound life lessons that resonate with audiences decades after the films' release.

To understand Mr. Miyagi's essence, one must first look to his origins in Okinawa, Japan. Born in 1925 in Tomi Village, Okinawa, Miyagi's early life was steeped in the rich cultural traditions of the island. Okinawa, known for its unique blend of Japanese and Chinese influences, is the birthplace of karate. This environment undoubtedly shaped Miyagi's worldview and martial arts philosophy.

In Okinawa, Miyagi fell in love with a woman named Yukie. Their relationship, briefly explored in The Karate Kid Part II, offers a glimpse into Miyagi's capacity for deep, enduring love. However, their romance was cut short by circumstances that would lead Miyagi to leave his homeland.

Yumi Mita from Pixaba

The decision to leave Okinawa was a pivotal moment in Miyagi's life. While the exact reasons are not fully explored in the films, it's suggested that cultural expectations and family obligations played a role. This departure demonstrates Miyagi's courage in facing the unknown and his willingness to forge his own path, even at great personal cost.

Upon arriving in the United States, Miyagi's life took several dramatic turns. He enlisted in the U.S. Army during World War II, serving in the 442nd Infantry Regiment. This unit, composed primarily of Japanese

Americans, became the most decorated unit for its size and length of service in U.S. military history. Miyagi's service earned him the Medal of Honour, the highest military decoration in the United States.

This period of Miyagi's life showcases his bravery, loyalty, and willingness to serve a country that, at the time, was interning many Japanese Americans in camps. It speaks to his character and his ability to rise above prejudice and adversity.

However, Miyagi's life was marked by profound tragedy during this time. While he was serving overseas, his wife and newborn son died in the Manzanar internment camp due to complications during childbirth. This devastating loss would shape Miyagi's character, instilling in him a deep sense of grief but also a profound appreciation for life and compassion for others.

Central to Mr. Miyagi's character is his practice of Zen Buddhism and its integration with his martial arts philosophy. Zen, with its emphasis on mindfulness, self-discipline, and harmony with nature, permeates Miyagi's approach to both karate and life.

This is evident in his famous quote: "Wax on, wax off. Breathe in, breathe out. Wax on, wax off. Don't forget to breathe, very important." Here, Miyagi encapsulates the Zen concept of mindfulness in everyday tasks, teaching that even mundane activities can be a form of meditation and training.

Miyagi's karate style, while fictional, draws heavily from traditional Okinawan martial arts, particularly Goju-Ryu. His emphasis on defence rather than aggression, and on personal development rather than competition, aligns with the original intent of karate as a means of self-improvement and self-defence.

One of Miyagi's most notable hobbies is the cultivation of bonsai trees. This Japanese art form, which involves growing and shaping miniature trees, serves as a metaphor for many of Miyagi's life philosophies. Bonsai requires patience, attention to detail, and a deep respect for nature – all qualities that Miyagi embodies and seeks to instill in his students.

In one poignant scene, Miyagi explains to Daniel LaRusso: "Close eye. Trust. Concentrate. Think only tree. Make perfect picture down to last pine needle. Wipe mind clean everything but tree. Nothing exists in whole world... only tree. You got it? Open eye." This lesson in visualization and focus extends far beyond bonsai or karate, teaching the power of concentration and clarity of mind in all aspects of life.

Another intriguing aspect of Miyagi's character is his collection of classic cars. This hobby reveals several facets of his personality: his appreciation for craftsmanship, his connection to history, and his ability to see value in things others might overlook. It also serves as a bonding point between Miyagi and Daniel, highlighting Miyagi's role as not just a sensei, but a father figure and friend.

Miyagi's approach to car restoration mirrors his philosophy on personal growth. As he tells Daniel, "First learn stand, then learn fly. Nature rule, Daniel-san, not mine." This patience and respect for process applies equally to restoring a vintage automobile and developing oneself as a martial artist and human being.

Mr. Miyagi's wisdom offers numerous lessons that remain relevant in today's fast-paced, often chaotic world:

Balance in all things: Miyagi's famous crane kick stance is a physical representation of his philosophy of balance. In life, he teaches the importance of balancing work and play, action and reflection, strength and gentleness.

Respect and compassion: Despite facing discrimination and personal tragedy, Miyagi maintains a deep respect for others and a compassionate outlook. His treatment of others, regardless of their background or actions, serves as a powerful example of empathy and understanding.

The power of mentorship: Miyagi's relationship with Daniel demonstrates the profound impact a positive mentor can have on a young person's life. In an era where many youth lack strong role models, Miyagi's approach to mentorship is particularly poignant.

Perseverance in the face of adversity: Miyagi's life story is one of overcoming tremendous obstacles. His resilience in the face of war, discrimination, and personal loss is inspirational and teaches the importance of maintaining one's principles and moving forward despite life's challenges.

The integration of philosophy and action: Miyagi doesn't just preach his beliefs; he lives them. His actions consistently align with his words, demonstrating the importance of integrity and walking one's talk.

Lifelong learning: Despite his mastery, Miyagi never presents himself as having all the answers. His humility and continued pursuit of knowledge and skill serve as a reminder that growth is a lifelong process.

The value of tradition and innovation: Miyagi respects tradition deeply but isn't bound by it. He adapts his teaching methods to suit Daniel's needs, showing the importance of flexibility and innovation while honouring one's roots.

Mr. Miyagi's enduring popularity among martial artists and the general public alike speaks to the universal appeal of his character and teachings.

For modern martial arts practitioners, Miyagi represents an ideal that goes beyond mere physical technique. He embodies the true spirit of martial arts as a path to personal growth, self-discipline, and harmony with oneself and others.

In an era where martial arts are often commercialised or reduced to sport, Miyagi's holistic approach serves as a reminder of the deeper philosophical and spiritual aspects of these disciplines. His emphasis on character development over tournament victories resonates with practitioners who seek more than just physical skills from their training.

In today's world, where the pursuit of quick results often overshadows the value of patient effort, where conflict often trumps compassion, and where the deeper meanings of martial arts are sometimes lost in the pursuit of trophies or belts, Mr. Miyagi stands as a beacon. He reminds us of the power of mentorship, the importance of balance, and the potential for martial arts to be a transformative practice that extends far beyond the dojo.

For martial artists, educators, parents, and individuals seeking personal growth, Mr. Miyagi offers a template of wisdom, compassion, and strength. His legacy continues to inspire, challenging us to look beyond the surface, to find balance in our lives, and to approach both our training and our daily existence with mindfulness, respect, and an open heart.

In the words of Mr. Miyagi himself, "Whole life have a balance. Everything be better." As we navigate the complexities of the modern world, we would do well to remember these words and the timeless wisdom they represent.

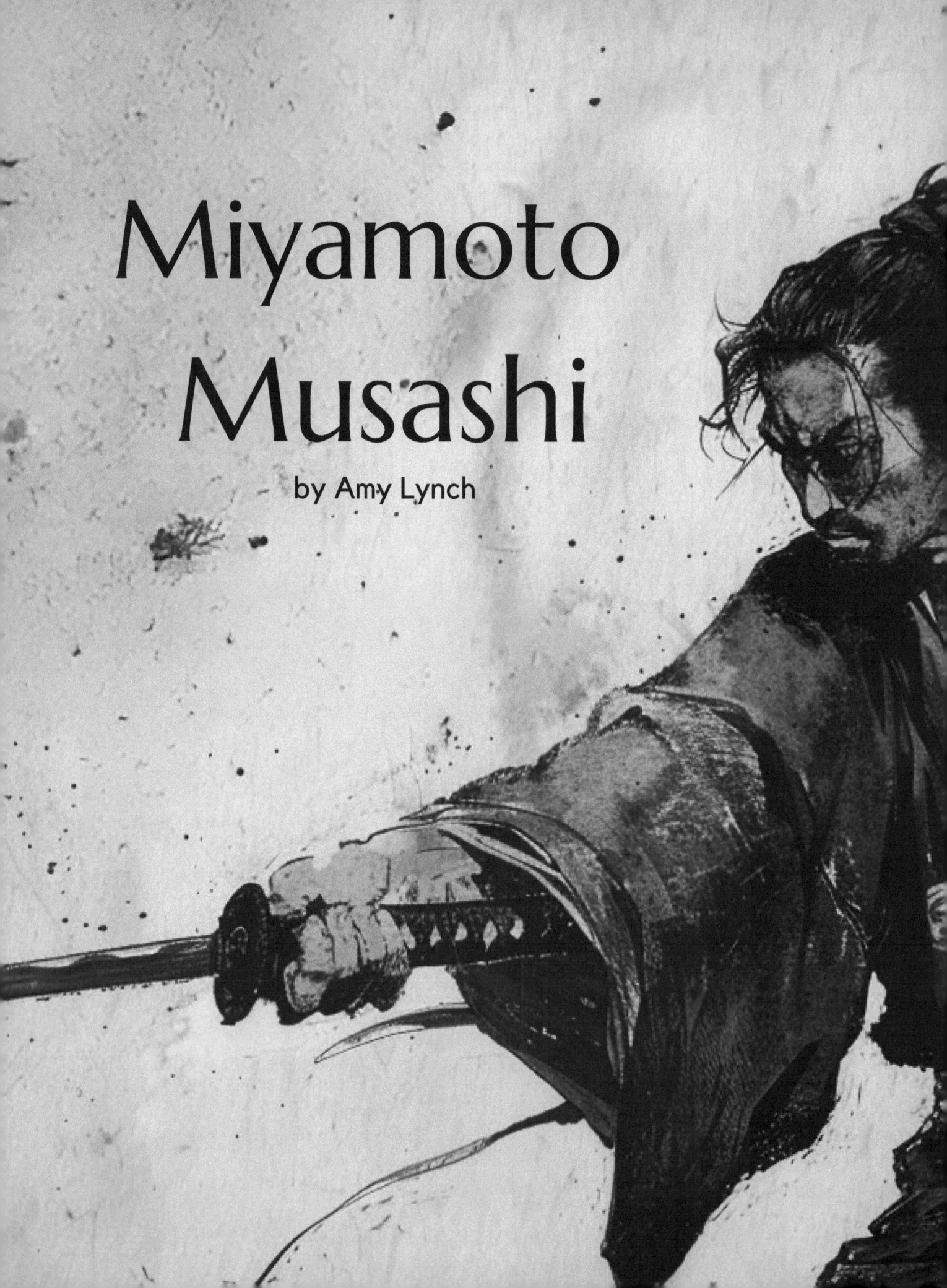

Miyamoto Musashi

by Amy Lynch

In 1612, Miyamoto Musashi, already a renowned swordsman, was challenged to a duel by Sasaki Kojiro, another famous samurai. Kojiro was known for his 'swallow cut' a technique of cutting a bird in flight, and wielded a nodachi, an oversized sword.

The duel was set to take place on a small island between the main Japanese island of Honshu and the island of Kyushu. Musashi arrived late, a tactic he often employed to unnerve his opponents. But what truly shocked everyone was his choice of weapon.

Instead of his usual two swords, Musashi appeared with only a wooden sword (bokken) that he had carved from an oar on his boat ride to the island. This wooden sword was slightly longer than a standard katana, giving Musashi a reach advantage.

Kojiro, insulted by Musashi's late arrival and unconventional weapon choice, drew his sword in anger. Musashi remained calm, using Kojiro's irritation to his advantage. As they faced off, Kojiro made the first move, slashing at Musashi with his famous swallow cut.

Musashi, however, was prepared. He deftly avoided the strike and countered with a powerful blow to Kojiro's head using his wooden sword. Some accounts say he struck Kojiro's forehead, while others claim he crushed Kojiro's rib cage. Regardless of the exact point of impact, the blow was fatal, and Kojiro fell.

Having won the duel, Musashi quickly returned to his boat and left the island, wary of retaliation from Kojiro's supporters. This duel became one of the most famous in samurai history, highlighting Musashi's strategic genius and unconventional thinking.

The use of a wooden sword against a real blade demonstrated Musashi's supreme confidence and skill. It also embodied his philosophy that the mind and strategy are more important than the weapon itself. This event contributed significantly to Musashi's legendary status in Japanese martial arts history.

This story, while based on historical events, has been romanticised over time. It's often used to illustrate the principles Musashi later wrote about in his famous text, "The Book of Five Rings," emphasizing strategy, psychology, and adaptability in combat and in life.

Miyamoto Musashi's "The Book of Five Rings" (Go Rin No Sho) is a classic text on martial strategy, philosophy, and tactics. Written in the early 17th century, it outlines Musashi's approach to combat and life. The book is divided into five chapters, each representing an element: Earth, Water, Fire, Wind, and Void. Here are the key principles Musashi wrote about:

The Way of Strategy:
Musashi emphasises that the way of the warrior (bushido) should be a way of life, not just a set of combat techniques. He stresses the importance of continuous learning and self-improvement.

Adaptability:
Like water taking the shape of its container, a warrior should be adaptable to any situation. This principle applies to both combat tactics and life strategies.

Perceiving the Whole:
Musashi advocates for a holistic view in combat and in life. Understanding the bigger picture allows for better decision-making and strategy.

The Importance of Timing:
Proper timing is crucial in combat and in life. Knowing when to act and when to wait is a key skill.

The Void (Emptiness):
This concept refers to the state of detachment from earthly desires and emotions, allowing for clear perception and action.

Practical Approach:
Musashi emphasises practicality over theory. He believes in learning through experience and real-world application.

The Importance of Strategy:
Musashi emphasises that strategy should guide all actions, both in combat and in life.

Psychological Warfare:
Understanding and manipulating the opponent's mind is as important as physical combat.

Simplicity:
Musashi advocates for simplicity in technique and lifestyle. He believes that complexity can be a hindrance.

The Single Cut:
The idea that a single, well-executed action is often more effective than multiple, less focused efforts.

Weapons Mastery:
While focusing on swordsmanship, Musashi emphasises the importance of mastering various weapons and understanding their applications.

The Body and Mind Connection:
Musashi stresses the importance of training both the body and the mind, viewing them as interconnected.

Observation and Perception:
Keen observation of oneself, the opponent, and the environment is crucial for success.

Rhythm and Tempo:
Understanding and controlling the rhythm of combat (and by extension, life) is a key principle.

Continuous Improvement:
The path of the warrior is one of lifelong learning and refinement.

These principles, while rooted in martial arts, are often applied to business, sports, and personal development in modern times. Musashi's work continues to be studied not just for its martial insights, but for its broader philosophical approach to life and conflict.

Miyamoto Musashi's approach, as outlined in The Book of Five Rings, has both strengths and weaknesses, especially when viewed through a modern lens. Let's examine the good and bad aspects of his philosophy and consider its validity today:

The Good:

1. Emphasis on Continuous Learning: Musashi's insistence on lifelong learning and self-improvement is highly relevant in today's rapidly changing world.

2. Adaptability: The principle of being flexible and adaptable is crucial in modern times, both in business and personal life.

3. Holistic Perspective: Seeing the bigger picture and understanding the interconnectedness of things is valuable in complex modern systems.

4. Practical Approach: Focusing on practical application rather than just theory is beneficial in many fields.

5. Mindfulness and Self-awareness: The concept of 'void' or clarity of mind is similar to modern mindfulness practices.

6. Strategic Thinking: The emphasis on strategy and long-term planning is crucial in today's competitive environments.

The Bad:

1. Violence-Centric: Much of Musashi's philosophy is rooted in combat, which may not directly translate to peaceful modern contexts.

2. Individualistic Focus: There's less emphasis on teamwork and collaboration, which are crucial in many modern settings.

3. Gender Bias: As a product of its time, the text doesn't address gender equality, which is a critical issue today.

4. Lack of Ethical Framework: While it touches on personal conduct, it doesn't provide a comprehensive ethical system for modern complexities.

5. Potential for Misinterpretation: Some might misuse concepts like psychological warfare in harmful ways in personal or professional settings.

6. Cultural Specificity: Some concepts are deeply rooted in feudal Japanese culture and may not translate well to all modern contexts.

Validity Today:

Many of Musashi's core principles remain valid and applicable today:

1. Adaptability and continuous learning are crucial in the modern, fast-paced world.

2. Strategic thinking and understanding the 'big picture' are valuable in business and personal life.

3. The emphasis on practical experience over pure theory is relevant in many fields.

4. Concepts like timing, rhythm, and balance apply to many aspects of modern life, from business negotiations to personal relationships.

5. The idea of mastering one's craft thoroughly is respected in various professions.

6. Psychological insights about understanding oneself and others remain valuable.

application of these principles in modern contexts requires careful interpretation:

1. The focus on individual achievement should be balanced with the importance of teamwork and collaboration.

2. The martial emphasis needs to be translated into non-violent contexts.

3. Ethical considerations and inclusivity need to be added to make the philosophy more comprehensive and applicable in diverse, modern settings.

4. The cultural context needs to be understood, and principles should be adapted rather than adopted wholesale.

While many of Musashi's core ideas remain relevant, they need to be critically examined and adapted to fit modern ethical standards and societal needs. The enduring value of "The Book of Five Rings" lies in its strategic thinking and philosophical approach to mastery and self-improvement, rather than its specific tactical advice for combat.

24 - The Martial Artist
by Ben Ward

Let's pinpoint what it means to be a martial artist in the present-day world. I have identified five physical qualities, five personality qualities, five skill qualities, five practices and four points of Mastery in the Martial arts. Think of these things as aesthetic. They are a harmony of form that presents the martial artist as beauty.

Physical:
- Calluses
- 'Runner's head' or 'Gym head' of one's calf muscle
- No fat to slow down technique
- Superman/woman neck, matches the width of one's jaw
- 'V taper' - shoulder to waist ratio

Personalities:
- Charisma of the joker
- Charisma of the rebel
- Charisma of the moral code
- Charisma of the sixth sense
- Charisma of the prodigy

Skills:
- 4 minute km
- Good stretch
- High kicks
- Good sparrer or good self defence application
- Speed and power

Practices:
- Killer instinct
- Big eater, eats a lot at meals
- Ceremony such as to wake up get out of bed and drag a comb across their head
- Practice
- Worker - paid employment

Mastery:
- One hit one kill - hassai ikkatsu
- Humility in personality of a master, nonviolence, nothing ruffled, outsmart opponent without using strength
- 'Gunbaru' - To persevere to do one's best against odds
- Bunkai - hidden knowledge

These 24 qualities attribute a martial artist in today's world. The final four may not be achieved by every martial artist and only sometimes in a young martial artist and not all at once. But it is possible for a martial artist, man or woman to achieve all these qualities over a lifetime with hard work, discipline and heart.

It is impossible to deny that our lives are shaped by a multitude of influences and people in our lives. Some are people we are lucky enough to interact with every day and others are someone we have admired from a distance.

When I think about all the people who have inspired me in my life and especially as I have embarked on my martial arts journey. The first name that comes to mind is Ronda Rousey. She is known as one of best female fighters in the world and was the first U.S. woman to win a medal for Judo in the 2008 Olympic Games. She later became a top Women's Bantamweight fighter (which refers to UFC's female fighters 135 lbs and under). Also going on to dominate the WWE and on multiple occasions has won the ESPY's Award for Best Female Athlete. Throughout her illustrious career. Ronda has consistently been an inspiration for men and women, both inside and outside the ring.

Ronda's began her life as a fighter, she was born on the 1st February in 1987 and was born with the umbilical cord wrapped around her neck. Causing her to suffer from a condition called apraxia (making her unable to talk for six years). Then when she was eight, her father committed suicide from constant pain due to a spinal injury from a sledding accident. Later on in her teenage years, she endured a lot of bullying at school. No matter what she went through, she remained strong and confident. But due to all this, her mum took action and trained her in judo. Where she had instant success, leading the way to empower the people and the world around her.

One thing I admire about Ronda is today we live in a world that is full of judgment and body shaming. This is so evident in the media industry. I can relate to this as I had deal with body shaming from a young age from one of my own family members and barely ate because of this growing up. This is a horrible idealism of telling young girls they're not skinny enough and all that matters is how they look on the outside, but not who they are on the inside. Ronda once revealed she suffered from bulimia, and for years, she would hide it from her friends and family. Rousey explained that she ended her bulimic ways, because of help from her boyfriend, her fighting and her desire to be an inspiration to female athletes worldwide.

One of the biggest challenges she faced when training for the UFC was she had to overcome her body issues and learn to embrace her body type, instead of hating it. She said in an interview, "I grew up as an athlete doing judo, so I didn't really have a conventional, feminine body type. I grew up thinking that because my body type was uncommon (athletic) it was a bad thing. Now that I'm older, I've really begun to realise that I'm really proud that my body has developed for a purpose and not just to be looked at."

This is an extremely powerful mindset to have, showing future athletes, younger generations and anyone who has experienced a eating disorder. The importance of having a positive body image, eating healthy and showing they can be their own hero. They didn't need to be a certain weight to be classified as beautiful.

As a world-class martial artist, Rhonda trains anywhere from 2 to 3 training sessions per day. She discussed her motivation behind her training regime with Training Magazine. No matter the weather or how she feels, she knows that consistency in your training is key. This is something I wholeheartedly agree with, and I like to bring this mentality into my training as well. She once stated:

"There's no point in training if you're not having fun. I think I need to be mentally engaged and that's what makes me want to train longer – and it keeps it interesting. The trick is to make it an enjoyable experience and then motivation is easy to come by – and I really mean that. Embrace the training, because it hurts – and don't make excuses. I've done some great workouts in a hotel room, at the beach, in the gym. You can always do something. Come at it like, 'What am I doing today?–I'm pumped!' There's no routine really."

Because Ronda Rousey has been technically training since she was a young girl, she's had to endure her fair share of rivals and critics over the years. She has quoted saying "When I was in school, martial arts made you a dork, and I became self-conscious that I was too masculine. I was a 16-year-old girl with ringworm and cauliflower ears. People made fun of my arms and called me 'Miss Man.' It wasn't until I got older that I realised: These people are idiots. I'm fabulous."

As she got older and became more and more successful in her martial arts pursuits. She appears to have a new, refreshing view towards her critics. She said, in one of herpre-fight interviews with UFC.

"I'm not out to go and make 20,000-50,000 new friends. I'm just trying to do whatever I can to further my career, and if that involves accumulating some critics, they don't know me. They take a few fragments of information that they get about me and they make some sort of judgment about my character without even knowing me. And if someone that I'll never meet is making a wrong judgment about me from very little information, that's not really my problem at all. So I don't really feel that bad about it."

Regardless if you going through your martial arts or life's journey there is always going to be someone out there, telling you that you're not going to make it.

I have come across this many times, but I have learnt to use this as motivation to prove them wrong and not let them hold me back. As I like to say, "Never let someone who is too afraid of chasing their own dreams, talk you out of chasing yours."

Because she's been training nearly her whole life, she always continues to improve, adjusting her techniques and learning new skills in order to stay on top. I feel the same, that I continuously want to keep improving and learn new skills in order to become a more well rounded martial arts practitioner.

Many people either love her or hate her, Ronda has never shied away from being straightforward and bluntly honest with everything she has gone through. I feel she is judged so quickly just because of the media speculation.. You will find she has spoken openly about her struggles with bulimia, being homeless, and fear of losing fights.

"People say to me all the time, 'You have no fear,'" she told Esquire in a 2012 interview, "I tell them, No, that's not true. I'm scared all the time. You have to have fear in order to have courage. I'm a courageous person because I'm a scared person."

As the decades have gone by, more and more people are just now starting to take ownership of their self-confidence. And as the saying goes "confidence is key to your success". Ronda has been known to have a somewhat polarising viewpoint. She makes no apologies for her confidence, and has never been afraid to let her true self shine through. She once said, in an article in Fox Sports, "everything I've learned from fighting, I've been able to apply to my life outside of it. The main lesson I get from it: it taught me to be brave, and it taught me to value myself."

When asked what she thought when people were saying she was arrogant. She responded in the most beautiful way saying "Why is self confidence arrogant? Why is self-depreciation considered modesty? I worked my ass off to be able to have a high opinion of myself," Ronda said. "It took a long time and many, many years, and I'm never going to let anyone tell me that I should think less of myself."

Ronda Rousey loves spending time, raising awareness and donating to charities that mean a lot to her. One of her favourite charities is called "Don't throw up, Throw down" and donated $5,000 to this great cause and also has been raising awareness in mental health. Rousey is the true essence of what it means to fight "like a girl." Showing that no matter what obstacles get in your way, as long as you don't give up then you will succeed.

Rousey has even co-wrote her autobiography *My Fight Your Fight* with her sports journalist sister Maria Burns-Ortiz. Which delves into her journey from early childhood and entering in the UFC arena. And I have just finished her incredible 2nd autobiography called *Our Fight* which is about overcoming obstacles, challenges, defeat and how she rebuilt her life into something better in the aftermath. This clearly is a true inspiration of how not to give up even when giving up is all you want to do.

Also, she is mum to her daughter La'akea Makalapuaokalanipo Browne. As a mother myself, it is important to teach your kids to have that never give up attitude and if they put the work in. They will capable of achieving anything they put their heart and mind into. Never letting anyone to stop you from being who you are meant to be. I have loved training in martial arts with my sons and watching them transform into these incredible men.

When I look at a true hero and inspiration not only in my life but also in my martial arts journey. Ronda Rousey to me is empowerment, a symbol of strength, determination, and resilience for millions of women around the world. Despite relentless criticism and the obstacles she encountered, her determination inspires not only athletes but also all those who fight against adversity, who refuse to be defined by the limitations imposed by society today.

To me Ronda has shown incredible courage and strength. Making her in my eyes a true pioneer, a visionary who paves the way for a next generation of strong and confident women. She shows the world that nothing is impossible for those who dare to chase their dreams. And reminding us that we all have the power to overcome obstacles and become the heroes of our own stories, even when others' gazes are filled with judgment.

"I want to be the undisputed, best pound-for-pound woman in the world in MMA, and I want to do it while looking good and being entertaining. I want to bring women's MMA up to be just as respected as the men's. And I feel that if there's something you want to get done, you gotta do it yourself. I can't trust anybody else to do it for me, and I'm willing to put the work in and be that person."

BEEF & VEGETABLE SLOW COOKER SOUP

Ingredients:
500g lean beef, cubed
1 onion, diced
2 carrots, sliced
2 celery stalks, chopped
2 potatoes, cubed
1 cup sliced green beans
1 can diced tomatoes
6 cups beef stock
2 cloves garlic, minced
1 bay leaf
1 tsp dried thyme
Salt and pepper to taste

Instructions:
Place all ingredients in the slow cooker.
Stir to combine.
Cover and cook on low for 8 hours or on high for 4 hours.
Remove bay leaf before serving.

This soup is rich in protein from the beef, complex carbohydrates from the vegetables, and various vitamins and minerals. It's perfect for post-training recovery and can be easily prepared in advance.

Pumpkin Soup

Ingredients:

1 medium pumpkin - 750g peeled and cubed
1 onion, diced
2 cloves garlic, minced
2 carrots, chopped
1 apple, peeled and chopped
4 cups vegetable broth
1 cup coconut milk
2 tbsp olive oil
1 tsp ground cinnamon
1/2 tsp ground nutmeg
Salt and pepper to taste
Pumpkin seeds for garnish (optional)

Instructions:
1. Heat olive oil in a large pot over medium heat. Add onion and garlic, sauté until softened.
2. Add pumpkin, carrots, and apple. Cook for 5 minutes, stirring occasionally.
3. Pour in vegetable broth. Bring to a boil, then reduce heat and simmer for 20-25 minutes until vegetables are tender.
4. Add cinnamon, nutmeg, salt, and pepper.
5. Use an immersion blender to puree the soup until smooth. Alternatively, carefully transfer to a blender in batches.
6. Stir in coconut milk and heat through.
7. Serve hot, garnished with pumpkin seeds if desired.

Write for Us

We want your authentic story, your journey and the reason WHY you love what you do. Below is a list of suggested topics. It is not exhaustive, so if you have an idea that we haven't come up with yet, drop us a line: training tips; technique workshops; style origins; kids in ma; training fuel; style anatomy; family pages; instructor profile; keeping it real; and more...

We are a quarterly magazine that celebrates and inspires a broad community of Martial Artists across the country. Our goal is to support all MA practitioners. Both instructors and students are encouraged to share their personal experiences, triumphs, and challenges within the style they love.

We feature interviews, rants, research, photography, projects and editorials that are respectful to all styles and are keeping in line with our magazine's inclusive philosophy.

Just as no two styles of Martial Arts are alike, our writers should have their own unique voice and tell their story from their own perspective. We encourage you to speak your truth.

Don't worry if you feel that your writing is not up to scratch, just tell us your story, your tip or your instruction the best way you can and our in-house editor will do the rest.

Email your submissions to info@martialartsmagazineaustralia.com (text in .doc) and (photos in JPEG).